*The Heart Healthy Cookbook for Two*

# *The* Heart Healthy
## COOKBOOK FOR TWO

125 Perfectly Portioned, Low-Sodium, Low-Fat Recipes

Jennifer Koslo, PhD, RDN, CSSD

callisto
publishing
an imprint of Sourcebooks

# Contents

# Foreword

**Cardiovascular disease is the leading cause of death for American men and women,** and a major contributor to disability and financial hardship. As a cardiologist in a busy and diverse suburban practice, I see the consequences of advanced heart disease in my exam room and hospital every day. Yet medical research from the Centers for Disease Control estimates that as many as 80 percent of heart disease deaths are preventable simply by adopting a heart healthy lifestyle and getting routine medical care when needed. These lifesaving habits include a heart-smart diet, regular exercise, maintaining a healthy body weight, alcohol in moderation when appropriate, and not smoking.

After a heart attack occurs, simply switching to a healthier diet may lower the risk of a second event by more than 50 percent compared to standard medical care alone. Diet and lifestyle also have a powerful influence on your likelihood of developing cancer, dementia, diabetes, arthritis, lung disease, and many other health conditions.

Although rapid treatment of heart attacks and other critical cardiac illnesses is a prime focus of cardiology training, I have come to appreciate the power of the small but vital lifestyle choices that we make every day. For the past 20 years, I have made prevention a cornerstone of my practice. And while people may sometimes balk at the idea of pharmaceutical treatment, I have found that nothing creates more confusion and anxiety than a recommendation to change eating habits.

What's holding you back? In many cases, it is fear of the unknown. Fear of giving up flavor and pleasure, and fear of having to learn complicated and time-consuming new culinary skills. Maybe it's just fear of boring food. Well, fear not. You're in for a treat.

Jennifer Koslo's recipes are delicious, easy to follow, and super healthy. She uses simple ingredients to create imaginative meals with sophisticated flavors. Southwestern, Asian, Italian, even Moroccan cuisine are all included, alongside such all-American choices as hash browns and tomato basil soup. It's nearly impossible to choose a favorite recipe, but broiled tuna steaks with peppercorn lime rub, asparagus fries, and dark chocolate avocado mousse all caught my fancy. What's more, Koslo will teach you cooking techniques

you may not have considered, such as baking in parchment or using your slow cooker to create a delicious meal with minimum fuss.

These are recipes that will serve you well on almost any occasion, and in portions that are just right. So many cookbook authors assume that the reader is cooking for a crowd, whereas the US Census Bureau reports that over 60 percent of households consist of one or two people. The recipes you will find in *The Heart Healthy Cookbook for Two* are perfect for sharing with a friend or loved one, or making for yourself with leftovers to spare. I especially appreciate the inclusion of recommendations for side dishes, and tips to avoid wasting ingredients.

Whether you have already embraced a healthy diet and are simply looking for new adventures in cooking, or perhaps trying to turn your health around, *The Heart Healthy Cookbook for Two* is a wonderful resource. In these pages, you will find a world of fabulously delicious meals that will nourish heart and soul, along with sound advice for achieving optimal health through smart and simple everyday choices.

—Sarah Samaan, MD, FACC
Author of *Best Practices for a Healthy Heart:
How to Stop Heart Disease Before or After It Starts*

# Introduction

**Heart health is something every American should be concerned about.** Heart disease (and its most common form, coronary artery disease, or CAD) is the leading cause of death for both men and women in the United States, and stroke is the fifth most common cause of death. Cardiovascular disease is often referred to as "the silent killer" because there may not be any warning signs before a heart attack strikes. Fortunately, a healthy heart is within your control. And while many risk factors for heart disease, such as age and family history, can't be changed, you can limit these risks, and others, by making healthy lifestyle choices. Unfortunately, many people are not using lifestyle habits to their advantage, for a variety of reasons including lack of time, lack of knowledge, or lack of motivation and commitment. Your lifestyle is your best defense against heart disease and stroke, and with every action you take to protect your heart, your overall health will get a boost too.

Over the years in my practice as a registered dietitian nutritionist, I have worked with many men and women diagnosed with heart disease and high blood pressure; high-risk people with two (or more) chronic illnesses at the same time, including diabetes and obesity; people who have suffered a heart attack or stroke; and people recovering from heart procedures. In many of these cases patients were left shocked, scared, and with-out the knowledge or necessary support to get their health back on track. Luckily, most people fully recover after a heart attack or procedure. However, it is important to imme-diately take steps to control, modify, or eliminate risk factors including hypertension, diabetes, elevated cholesterol, smoking, obesity, and lack of physical activity. Even just one risk factor will raise your chances of having heart-related problems.

There are many strategies that can protect your heart and virtually eliminate your risk of heart disease. Don't wait until you have experienced a heart attack before you take action; make a commitment today to move forward with a heart healthy lifestyle. I wrote this book for the many men and women who are dealing with the challenges of heart-related issues, because a healthy diet is one of your best weapons against heart disease.

The foods you eat affect your modifiable risk factors including your weight, cholesterol, blood pressure, and risk for diabetes. The recipes and information in this book illustrate how to choose a nutrient-rich heart healthy diet: high in vitamins, minerals, fiber, and phytochemicals; emphasizing vegetables, fruits, and whole grains; including low-fat dairy products, poultry, fish, legumes, nontropical oils, and nuts; and limiting the use of sugar, sodium, and red meat.

Regardless of where you are in terms of heart health, you can begin today by implementing lifestyle changes—like writing a healthy list for your next grocery visit or going for a walk at lunch time—that focus on taking small manageable steps toward improving your heart health.

# 1

# The Heart of the Matter

*For someone with heart disease, diet is an important topic. Along with other healthy habits like not smoking and being physically active, the right type of eating plan can slow or even partially reverse the narrowing of the heart's arteries and help prevent further complications. You may already be somewhat familiar with what a "heart healthy" diet is. However, based on the most recent research, there have been some subtle yet important changes to those recommendations, which may actually be welcome news.*

# What Does "Heart Healthy" Really Mean?

With the release of the 2013 American Heart Association and American College of Cardiology "Guideline on Lifestyle Management to Reduce Cardiovascular Risk" (Eckel, et al., 2013) and the 2015–2020 Dietary Guidelines for Americans there has been a shift toward *dietary patterns* rather than single nutrients or food groups. The nutrition "biggies" never change: eat more fruits and vegetables, eat more whole grains, choose lean proteins, enjoy foods in moderation. However, you may want to be sitting down for the latest official advice on cholesterol: Based on the available evidence, dietary cholesterol *does not* play a major role in blood cholesterol, therefore dietary cholesterol limits have been removed from current guidelines. What *does* play a role in raising blood cholesterol is dietary trans fat and saturated fat. We still need to eat fats, but we are encouraged to be more aware of the types of fats we eat and less about the total amount of fat we eat.

So what do the experts recommend? For cardiovascular disease prevention, joint guidelines recommend consuming a dietary pattern that emphasizes the consumption of vegetables, fruits, and whole grains; includes low-fat dairy products, poultry, fish, legumes, nontropical vegetable oils, and nuts; and limits the intake of sodium, sweets, sugar-sweetened beverages, and red meats. A heart healthy diet should:

- limit saturated fat intake to 5 to 6 percent of total calories;

- reduce the percentage of calories from saturated and trans fats;

- keep sodium intake to less than 2,300 milligrams per day; 1,500 milligrams per day for those with prehypertension, hypertension, and/or at high risk for atherosclerotic cardiovascular disease; and

- limit the intake of added sugars to less than 10 percent of total calories per day.

This type of eating pattern can be achieved by following the Dietary Approaches to Stop Hypertension (DASH), the United States Department of Agriculture eating plan (ChooseMyPlate), a Mediterranean eating plan, or plans endorsed by the American Heart Association (including DASH, Therapeutic Lifestyle Change diet (TLC), and the Mediterranean eating plan). What is most important to remember is: **these are not diets nor fads;** but *evidence-based healthy dietary patterns* and a plan for eating whole foods to decrease the risk of chronic disease. It's all about the interaction of the many beneficial vitamins, minerals, antioxidants, zoochemicals, and phytochemicals found in whole, unprocessed foods.

Here is an overview of how the top-ranked heart healthy eating plans compare.

| | DASH Eating Plan | Mediterranean Eating Plan | Therapeutic Lifestyle Change Diet (TLC) | Plant-Based (Vegan) Eating Plan |
|---|---|---|---|---|
| The Aim | Lowering blood pressure, lowering LDL | Weight loss, heart and brain health, cancer prevention, and diabetes control and prevention | Reducing cholesterol | Improving overall health, preventing chronic disease, and possible weight loss |
| Dietary Pattern Emphasis | Whole grains, fruits, vegetables, low-fat dairy, nuts, fish, poultry, and legumes. Low in sodium, red meat, and sugar | Primarily plant-based: high intake of vegetables, fruits, whole grains, beans, nuts and seeds, herbs, and spices. Olive oil primary source of fat. High intake of fish; low intake of dairy, poultry, and red meat. Moderate consumption of wine | Whole grains, fruits, vegetables, low-fat dairy, nuts, fish, poultry, and legumes. Low in sodium, red meat, and sugar. The key is cutting back sharply on saturated fat and trans fat, and increasing dietary fiber | Whole grains, fruits, vegetables, nuts, and legumes. No animal products (dairy, eggs, fish, meats, and poultry) |
| Will You Lose Weight? | Though not originally designed as a weight-loss diet, you will likely lose weight if you follow the DASH plan and include exercise. | While some research links the Mediterranean diet to weight loss, the jury is still out. It is important to note that exercise is a central part of this lifestyle. | The diet was designed to lower cholesterol levels, not for weight loss, but research suggests that lower-fat diets tend to promote weight loss. | Likely, as vegans tend to eat fewer calories when following a balanced, well-planned plant-based diet |
| How Easy Is It to Follow? | DASH doesn't restrict entire food groups but it may initially be difficult to transition to a diet lower in fat, salt, and sugar. | Because the Mediterranean pattern doesn't ban food groups, it should be easy to follow long term. | It may require some initial work and an increased aptitude for label reading to ensure that you keep your saturated fat intake to less than 7 percent of calories. | Veganism requires planning, especially if you are new to this style of eating. |

## Conforming to Heart Healthy Guidelines

The recipes in this book conform to heart healthy dietary patterns by focusing on the use of whole, unprocessed ingredients. Tropical oils such as coconut oil are not used, sodium levels are kept in check, and none of the recipes contain added trans fats. An important note is that the recipes are not nonfat; in fact they all include a source of healthy fat, which is an essential nutrient used by the body for many important processes. Oils from plant sources are more than just fats: they contain many antioxidants and phytonutrients and there are numerous cardioprotective benefits to replacing saturated fats with mono-unsaturated fats and polyunsaturated fats.

## Crossover Conditions

Heart healthy eating plans are also beneficial for other health conditions. These eating plans target people who:

- carry their excess weight around their middle (central belly fat);
- have metabolic syndrome;
- have high triglycerides;
- have prediabetes, diabetes, prehypertension, or hypertension;
- are postmenopausal; or
- have polycystic ovarian syndrome.

Eating a whole-foods, mostly plant-based diet and including daily activity is the best way for men and women of all ages to improve their health and lower their risk for developing chronic disease.

## Going Low

Focusing on diet quality is a cornerstone of a heart healthy diet. For the most part, you should think more in terms of what you can *add* to make your diet more nutrient dense, rather than what you have to limit. There are, however, some nutrients you do need to keep in check, and having a better understanding of what that means will make it easier for you to do this.

- **Sodium:** For optimal heart health, the American Heart Association recommends that people aim to eat no more than 1,500 milligrams of sodium per day. This is the level associated with a significant reduction in blood pressure, which in turn reduces the risk for heart disease. Most of the sodium Americans eat comes from processed, packaged, and restaurant foods—not from the saltshaker—so preparing your own meals is one of the easiest ways to lower the amount of sodium in your diet.

- **Dietary fats:** Dietary fats are essential to give your body energy and support cell growth. They also help your body absorb fat-soluble vitamins, protect your organs, and keep you warm. The American Heart Association recommends limiting saturated and trans fats and replacing them with healthier monounsaturated fats and polyunsaturated fats. If you have high cholesterol, you should reduce your daily saturated fat intake to no more than 5 to 6 percent of total calories. For someone on a 2,000-calorie diet, that equates to 13 grams of saturated fat per day.

There are two main types of potentially harmful dietary fats:

- **Saturated fat:** This type comes mainly from animal sources, is solid at room temperature (think butter and lard), and raises LDL (bad) cholesterol.

- **Trans fat:** While there are some naturally occurring trans fats, most are made through a processing method called partial hydrogenation. These fats increase LDL cholesterol, lower HDL (good) cholesterol, and increase your risk for heart disease. These are by far the most harmful type of fat.

The three main types of healthy dietary fats are mostly unsaturated:

- **Monounsaturated fats:** This type is found in vegetable oils and a variety of foods like avocados and nuts. Foods rich in monounsaturated fats can improve blood cholesterol levels, which can lower risk for heart disease, and they may also lower insulin levels, which can be beneficial for people with type 2 diabetes. Monounsaturated fats include olive, canola, peanut, and sesame oils.

- **Polyunsaturated fats:** This type is found in plant-based foods and oils. Eating foods rich in polyunsaturated fats may improve blood cholesterol levels and lower risk for heart disease as well as type 2 diabetes. Polyunsaturated fats include soybean, safflower, corn, and sunflower oils.

- **Omega-3 fats:** This is a type of polyunsaturated fatty acid that may be especially beneficial to the heart. Omega-3s, such as those found in fish, appear to lower the risk for heart disease.

Eating foods with fat is definitely part of a heart healthy diet. Don't eliminate them from your diet; instead, focus on replacing saturated and trans fats with healthier monounsaturated and polyunsaturated fats, and balance the amount of calories you eat from all foods with the amount of calories you burn.

Aiming for a dietary pattern that emphasizes the intake of vegetables, fruits, and whole grains; includes low-fat dairy products, poultry, fish, legumes, nontropical oils. and nuts; and limits the intake of sodium, sweets, sugar-sweetened beverages, and red meats will mean your diet is low in both saturated fat and trans fat.

## Fighting with Fiber

Fruits, vegetables, and whole grains contain dietary fiber, which can influence many aspects of health. From gut bacteria to weight loss, fiber is a fundamental part of a healthy diet. There are two main types of fiber: **soluble** (blends with water in the gut to form a gel-like substance) and **insoluble** (does not blend with water and passes through the digestive tract mostly intact). It's important to have both in your diet, and luckily, most fiber-rich plant foods contain a mixture of both.

Beans, fruits, and oats are especially good sources of **soluble fiber**. This is the type of fiber that can help lower cholesterol, increase feelings of fullness, and control blood sugar by slowing down nutrient digestion and absorption.

Whole grains, nuts, seeds, and vegetables are all good sources of **insoluble fiber,** which, because it remains mostly intact as it passes through the digestive tract, increases fecal bulk and helps prevent constipation.

Aim for 25 to 35 grams of total fiber each day (11 grams per 1,000 calories), or 6 to 8 grams per meal, and 3 to 4 grams per snack, choosing from a mix of foods containing both soluble and insoluble fiber.

## Rethinking Your Kitchen Staples

Eating less sodium, saturated fat, trans fat, and sugar, and eating more fruits, vegetables, and whole grains will boost your energy and improve your health. But beginning to make those changes to your eating habits can be daunting, especially if you aren't sure where to begin. Here are a few tips on how to transition to a more heart healthy diet:

- **Know that it's a process:** Making changes to your life, especially those surrounding foods and habits that have been in place for years, isn't going to happen

## *After the Attack*

A heart attack is a life-threatening medical condition in which the blood flowing to the heart suddenly stops, damaging the surrounding tissues. Most people survive a first heart attack and go on to lead a full life; however, adherence to the correct form of treatment is crucial to preventing future heart attacks. Typically, your doctor will refer you to a cardiac rehabilitation program where you can work with people who specialize in heart health. One of those people will be a registered dietitian nutritionist who will help you with dietary changes, and in most programs will also conduct cooking classes and demos, and give grocery store tours. If you have diabetes and obesity, you may be asked to lose weight and be put on a supervised exercise program. Post–heart attack dietary guidelines may need to be tailored for you depending on your medications and any additional chronic illnesses. In general, a post–heart attack diet is a lower-sodium heart healthy diet and should:

- be low in unhealthy trans and saturated fats,

- contain at least 4 to 5 cups of fruits and vegetables per day,

- have at least two (3.5-ounce) servings of fish per week,

- include at least three (1-ounce) servings of fiber-rich whole grains per day,

- be low in sodium (less than 1,500 milligrams per day),

- contain no more than 36 ounces of sugar-sweetened beverages per week, and

- include no processed meats.

overnight—and that's okay! Start with a few small, specific goals such as eating one additional vegetable serving each day, or learning to make three new healthy dinners in a month.

- **Do a pantry review:** Start by taking stock of the items you currently have in your pantry, refrigerator, and freezer. Make a note of foods that you currently eat that are processed. Read the ingredient labels and plan to donate or use up all items high in sugar, salt, and saturated fat. If any ingredient labels include "partially hydrogenated oils," the food contains trans fats (even if the nutrition facts states zero grams). You will want to toss those items.

- **Think about adding, not subtracting**: After you have decided which foods need to go, make a list of the whole foods with which you can replace the processed foods. It's really easy and super simple to always have fruits and vegetables on hand instead of prepackaged snacks. Place a bowl on your kitchen countertop and fill it with fresh fruit that you enjoy. Cut up vegetables like carrots, broccoli, cauliflower, and celery and store them in the refrigerator for easy snacking.

- **Go whole grain:** Stock up on healthier alternatives for foods you know and love. Swap your white rice and pasta for whole grains like brown rice, wild rice, whole-wheat couscous, quinoa, barley, buckwheat, millet, spelt, rolled oats, and amaranth.

- **Cook meals at home:** Cooking and preparing your meals at home is one of the best things you can do for your health. They will taste better and you will know exactly what ingredients are in your food. Plus, cooking is fun!

- **Try healthier condiments:** Ketchup and mustard can contain high amounts of sodium and sugar. Make your own condiments in Chapter 11 (page 187) and stock your pantry and refrigerator with a new assortment of nontraditional condiments like sriracha, curry powders, and hummus. Set the saltshaker aside and use either fresh or dried herbs or salt-free seasoning instead.

- **Choose cans carefully:** Many canned goods are high in salt and preservatives. Go with "no salt added" varieties and always drain and rinse vegetables and beans before using.

- **Enlist support:** Making a change is always easier and more enjoyable when you enlist the support of others. Swap recipes with friends and family members, go to the farmers' market with a friend, or find a "health" buddy to help you stay on track.

# Healthy Cooking Techniques

There are many ways to cook up juicy and flavorful foods without frying or adding unnecessary extras. By using healthy cooking techniques that eliminate excessive amounts of fats or salt, you can cut calories while retaining the nutrients and flavors in foods. Try preparing your favorite dishes using these healthy cooking methods:

- **Steaming:** To steam, place food in a perforated basket suspended above simmering liquid. The food will retain more flavor and won't need any salt. Foods that are great for this method are fish and chicken, and vegetables like broccoli, cauliflower, and green beans.

- **Poaching:** To poach, gently simmer food in a flavorful liquid such as low-sodium broth, wine, vinegar, or plain water with added herbs and spices, until the food is cooked through and tender. For stove-top poaching, choose a covered pan that best fits the size and shape of the food so you need a minimal amount of liquid. Poaching works well for fish, eggs, and poultry.

- **Broiling or grilling:** Both of these techniques expose food to direct heat. To grill outdoors, place the food on a grill rack above a bed of charcoal embers. If you have an indoor grill, follow the manufacturer's directions. To broil, place the food on a broiler rack below the heat source. Both methods allow fat to drip away from the food. These methods are great for chicken, fish, fruits, and vegetables.

- **Baking:** Baking generally doesn't require the use of added fats and you can bake seafood, meats, poultry, vegetables, and fruit, as well as desserts, breads, and quick breads. In addition to baking in a baking pan, you can enclose foods in a foil packet (or pouch) before baking in an oven. Pouching the food allows it to steam in the moisture coming from either the meat itself, or from the added broth, water, or wine.

- **Stir-frying:** A traditional Asian method, stir-frying quickly cooks small, uniformly sized pieces of food while they are rapidly stirred in a wok or large, nonstick frying pan. You need only a small amount of cooking spray or oil. Fish, pork, chicken, red meat, fruits, and vegetables all taste delicious using this method.

- **Roasting:** Roasting uses an oven's dry heat to cook food. The method is similar to baking, but typically the food is cooked at a higher temperature. Foods can be roasted on a baking sheet or in a roasting pan. For meats, poultry, and seafood, place them on a rack in the roasting pan so the fats can drip away.

- **Sautéing:** Sautéing generally involves the use of a nonstick pan so you use little to no oil when cooking, or a small amount of water, broth, or wine. This method quickly cooks relatively thin or small pieces of food such as red meat, chicken, fish, fruits, and vegetables.

Using fresh spices and herbs is one of the best ways to add color, taste, and aroma to foods without the use of salt or fat. Add fresh herbs toward the end of cooking and dried herbs in the earlier stages of cooking.

# Exercise

Regular exercise can help you control your weight, reduce your risk of heart disease, strengthen your bones and muscles, and lower stress levels. But if it's been a while since you have been active, or you have been recently diagnosed with heart disease, have diabetes or other co-morbidities (kidney disease, etc.), are a male over the age of 40, or a female over the age of 50, it is important to obtain medical clearance from your physician before starting an exercise program.

Most adults, if healthy enough for exercise, can start a moderate-intensity program, such as briskly walking for 30 minutes per day, with little risk. The 2008 Physical Activity Guidelines for Americans (*Health.gov*/ODPHP) recommends the following: 150 minutes of moderate-intensity aerobic activity (e.g., brisk walking) or 75 minutes of vigorous aerobic activity (e.g., running) per week, and muscle-strengthening activities on two or more days of the week that work all major muscle groups (legs, hips, back, abdomen, chest, shoulders, and arms).

While 150 minutes a week sounds like a lot, the good news is that you can be active in short 10-minute bouts to accumulate your 2 hours and 30 minutes throughout the week. Even better, just about any type of activity counts. Here are some tips for fitting activity into a busy schedule:

- Go for a short walk (about 10 minutes) before breakfast, at lunchtime, and after dinner.

- "House walk" (a more enjoyable sounding term than "pacing") while you are talking on the phone.

- When walking, pick up the pace from leisurely to brisk.

- Take the stairs instead of the elevator, park at the farther end of the parking lot, and walk every aisle at the grocery store.

- Take your dog on longer walks, or volunteer at an animal shelter to walk dogs.

- Listen to music or watch your favorite shows while stretching and doing bodyweight exercises. You can even fit these exercises in during commercials.

- Do yard work, wash the car by hand, garden, or make home repairs.

- Enlist support! Join an exercise group or organize daily neighborhood walks.

# 2

# Cooking for Two

*Sometimes cooking for two may seem like it's not worth the trouble. However, everyone needs a variety of foods to stay healthy, especially when trying to reduce the risk of developing chronic diseases like heart disease. Homemade meals are more nutritious, better tasting, and more economical than restaurant meals. In this chapter you will learn how to make the most of your meals for two.*

# Cooking Is Caring

Dealing with a health challenge such as heart disease can be scary, but learning new skills together with your partner can be both empowering and bonding. Together, you'll focus on adding heart-saving foods rather than foods that are off limits. It can be tricky when cooking for two to make the most of your ingredients and to minimize dishes, but just because you have a smaller household doesn't mean you should abandon the kitchen.

Each of the recipes in this book is designed to serve just two people. With recipes portioned for two, you won't have to worry about food waste or eating leftovers all week. Eating is a source of great enjoyment, so take time to savor the flavors, colors, and textures of a variety of foods.

## How to Plan for a Week

Planning makes all the difference when it comes to eating healthy meals. Set a goal to plan menus for a week at a time, choose your recipes, and prepare a shopping list that includes the quantities of each of the ingredients for the recipes you are planning to make. Be certain that your list includes healthy snacks to keep on hand in addition to the recipes you will prepare for breakfast, lunch, and dinner. Avoid the "there's nothing to eat" dilemma by keeping your pantry, refrigerator, and freezer stocked with healthy items. This will also cut down the temptation to eat unhealthy foods.

When shopping for two, the tendency is to buy too much, and what seems like a bargain is truly not because you end up throwing much of it out. An increasing number of supermarkets offer foods like grains, beans, seeds, nuts, spices, and dried fruits from bins rather than packages, which can help you buy only the amount you need. To cut down on food waste, if a recipe in this book calls for an ingredient that will yield an unused portion, the recipe will include a "Toss It Together Tip" to give you ideas on how to incorporate purchased items into other meals.

Lastly, when planning for the week, organize your kitchen so your equipment is within easy reach, and you have the tools you need. Read each recipe through in its entirety before beginning, taking note of the "prep" time, which is the time you need to spend chopping and preparing ingredients, and the "cook" time, which is the actual amount of time needed to cook the recipe.

With a little organization and effort, meal planning can help you and your partner eat healthier, slow the progression of heart disease, and save money.

# *Beyond Water*

Swapping out just one sugary drink per day can cut calories and lower your risk for heart disease and diabetes. Here are some healthy alternatives:

- **Flavored waters:** Many flavored waters still contain sugar or artificial sweeteners. A healthier alternative is natural flavoring: Add slices of your favorite fruits, vegetables, and herbs (lemons, oranges, cucumber, mint) to a pitcher of ice-cold water. Another option is to put chopped-up herbs and fruit in an ice cube tray, add water, and freeze.

- **Herbal teas:** All teas are rich in natural antioxidants and beneficial phytochemicals. Some good choices include green, white, and black. If you need to sweeten your tea, use just a few drops of stevia or choose a natural sweetener like honey.

- **Vegetables:** Vegetable juice offers a quick, low-calorie way to get many of the benefits of vegetables (with the exception of fiber) with far less sugar than fruit juices. But vegetable juices can be high in sodium, so opt for a low-sodium version or, better yet, make your own fresh juice at home with a juicer.

- **Plant-based milks:** Soy beverages are rich in cardioprotective phytonutrients and contain protein, vitamin D, and calcium with no saturated fat or cholesterol. Just choose varieties that contain little to no added sugar.

- **Red wine:** Red wine, when consumed in moderation, has been widely reported to reduce the risk of cardiovascular disease. The 2002-2020 Dietary Guidelines for Americans recommends that women limit consumption to one drink per day (5 ounces of wine), and men to two drinks per day, in order to reap the benefits.

# Perfectly Portioned

Each of the recipes in this book is perfectly portioned to serve two adults. Use the recipes to find your own healthy eating style that reflects your preferences, cultures, traditions, and budget so you can maintain it as a lifestyle. Each recipe has a nutritional breakdown so you can use the information to fit the recipes into your individualized eating plan. Everyone has different calorie needs based on age, gender, activity level, and whether a goal is weight gain or loss. The key is to choose a variety of foods from each group, making sure that each choice is limited in saturated fat, sodium, and added sugars.

| Food Group | Servings/Ounces for a 2,000-Calorie Diet | Examples of One Serving |
|---|---|---|
| **Grains: At least half your grains should be whole grains** | 6 to 8 ounces per day | • 1 slice bread<br>• 1 ounce dry cereal<br>• ½ cup cook pasta, rice or hot cereal |
| **Vegetables: Eat a variety of colors and types** | 4 to 5 servings per day | • 1 cup leafy vegetables<br>• ½ cup raw vegetables<br>• ½ cup vegetable juice |
| **Fruits: Eat a variety of colors and types** | 4 to 5 servings per day | • 1 medium fruit<br>• ¼ cup dried fruit<br>• ½ cup fruit juice |
| **Fat-free or low-fat dairy products** | 2 to 3 servings per day | • 1 cup fat-free or low-fat milk<br>• 1 cup fat-free or low-fat yogurt<br>• 1½ ounces cheese |
| **Lean meats, poultry, and seafood** | Less than 6 ounces per day | • 3 ounces cooked meat<br>• 3 ounces grilled fish |
| **Fats and oils: Use liquid oils most of the time** | 2 to 3 servings per day | • 1 teaspoon vegetable oil<br>• 1 teaspoon margarine (make sure there are no trans fats) |
| **Nuts, seeds, and legumes** | 4 to 5 servings per week | • ⅓ cup or 1½ ounces nuts<br>• 2 tablespoons peanut butter<br>• 2 tablespoons or ½ ounce seeds<br>• ½ cup dry beans or peas |
| **Sweets and added sugars** | 5 or fewer servings per week | • 1 tablespoon sugar<br>• 1 tablespoon jam<br>• 1 cup lemonade |

# 10 Ingredients to Keep on Hand

A well-stocked pantry, refrigerator, and freezer are key to staying on track with a heart healthy eating plan. With good, simple basics on hand, you can easily put together nutritious meals without reaching for processed foods or ordering take-out. The following are 10 foods used often in the recipes in this book that can make heart healthy eating nutritious and delicious.

1. **Olive oil and olive oil nonstick cooking spray:** Olive oil is one of the healthiest types of fats that you can use in your kitchen. It is a monounsaturated fat: the type of fat that can raise good (HDL) cholesterol and lower bad (LDL) cholesterol. To cut down on added calories, many recipes also call for the use of an olive oil nonstick cooking spray.

2. **Dried legumes and canned beans:** Dried lentils can be cooked in under 20 minutes and make a heart healthy addition to any meal. Canned beans are convenient and serve a variety of uses; just be certain to always drain and rinse them before using, to remove excess sodium and preservatives.

3. **Grains:** Whole grains, such as quinoa, millet, and brown rice, are a cornerstone of a heart healthy eating plan due to their fiber, vitamin, and mineral content. Stock your pantry with a variety of your favorites.

4. **Cereal grains:** Rolled oats, steel cut oats, oat bran: Oats are a heart's best friend as they are one of the richest sources of soluble fiber, the type of fiber that reduces bad (LDL) cholesterol.

5. **Frozen fruits and vegetables:** Frozen produce is as nutritious as fresh, maybe even more so as it is flash frozen when harvested to retain the maximum amount of nutrients. Read the labels and be certain you choose varieties without added sugars, sauces, or other ingredients.

6. **Eggs:** Eggs are an excellent source of complete, high-quality protein and can be used in a variety of ways. For added heart health benefits, choose eggs that have added omega-3 fats.

7. **Nuts:** Almonds, walnuts, and pistachios are full of heart healthy fats, vitamins, and minerals that can decrease your risk for disease. Choose unsalted and unseasoned varieties.

8. **Seeds:** Chia seeds and hemp seeds are particularly high in omega-3 fats and soluble fiber. They are used in a variety of recipes for added nutrition. Chia seeds can also be used as a smoothie thickener or egg replacer in baked goods.

9. **Greens:** Spinach and kale are powerhouses of nutrition and are used often in the recipes in this book. Choose prewashed greens to save time.

10. **Greek yogurt:** For heart health it is recommended to include 2 to 3 servings of low-fat or non-fat dairy products each day. Greek yogurt is an excellent source of protein, bone-strengthening vitamin D and calcium, and blood pressure–friendly potassium.

## Toss It Together

Whether you are cooking for 10 or 2, it's easy to end up wasting good food because you didn't plan well. These recipes are designed for two people, taking a lot of the guess-work out of how much to buy, helping you cut down on waste, and ultimately saving you money. These tips will also help you avoid food waste:

- Prepare a grocery list with the exact quantities of the ingredients you need: Live by the motto "buy what you need and eat what you buy." Check your pantry and fridge before you head to the store to make sure you are buying only what you need and no more.

- Buy fresh produce for one week at a time: Aim to go to the grocery store weekly and buy enough fresh produce to last that week.

- Make the freezer your friend: Freeze beans, bread, and leftover fruits and vegetables for later use. Freezing excess ingredients while the food is still fresh retains the most nutrients.

- Store food properly: Research how to properly store different foods. Some foods can be stored together while others need to be separated for a longer life. Note the shelf life of your pantry staples by reading the "use by" and "expires by" dates, and practice FIFO: "First in, first out," so you use the oldest foods first.

- Plan a "kitchen sink" meal every week: Still have a quarter of an onion or a couple of carrots? Plan one meal before the next grocery store trip that will use up leftover ingredients. The following table includes additional tips for using up those unused ingredients.

| Ingredient | Uses | Refrigerator Storage | Freezer Storage |
|---|---|---|---|
| **Fresh Greens** | Toss with a bowl of whole-wheat pasta and tuna for a quick lunch or dinner. | Wash, wrap in a paper towel, and store in plastic bags. | Roughly chop them and store in plastic bags for use in smoothies. |
| **Fresh Herbs** | Add to sandwiches, salads, cooked grains, and vegetables for added flavor. | Wash, pat dry, and store in resealable bags. | Chop finely, place in ice cube trays, and freeze. |
| **½ Onion** | Add to sandwiches, salads, cooked grains and vegetables for added nutrition. | Chopped or sliced onions can be stored in a sealed container for 3 to 4 days. | There is no need to blanch onions before freezing. Simply place them in a resealable bag and freeze. |
| **½ Banana** | Mash and use as an oil replacement in baked goods. Slice bananas and almonds for a healthy dessert or snack. | Store ripe bananas in the refrigerator to keep them perfect for a few extra days. | Slice bananas and freeze them in resealable bags to use in smoothies. |
| **Chia Seeds** | Toss chia seeds in salads and sprinkle over cooked vegetables for added crunch, fiber, and protein. | Chia seeds can be stored for months in a sealed container. | Chia seeds last for months in a sealed container. |
| **Cooked Grains** | Toss cooked grains with chopped vegetables, fresh herbs, vinegar, and oil. | Cooked grains can be stored in an airtight container for 3 to 5 days. | Freeze grains in resealable plastic bags in 2-cup portions. |
| **Nuts** | Sprinkle nuts over cooked hot cereals for an added nutritional boost. | Nuts can be stored in a sealed container for to up to a year. | Freeze nuts in resealable plastic bags for up to 2 years. |
| **Almond Milk** | Use for smoothies or enjoy a glass as a healthy alternative to soda. | Plant-based milks can generally be stored for 7 to 10 days. | Freeze almond milk in ice cube trays for perfect portions to use in smoothies. |
| **Greek Yogurt** | Top with berries and sliced nuts for a healthy breakfast or snack. | An opened container of Greek yogurt can be stored for 5 to 7 days. | Store for several months in airtight freezer bags to allow for expansion as the yogurt freezes. |
| **Cooked Beans** | Mix in beans with washed greens for a quick and healthy salad. | Cooked beans can be stored for 3 to 5 days. | Freeze beans in resealable plastic bags in 1-cup portions. |

## Suggested Meal Plan
## (First Month After Diagnosis)

The following table is a suggested one-month meal plan for embarking on a heart healthy diet. Use the weekly menus as a guide and feel free to swap out recipes or mix in your favorite low-sodium, low-fat favorites. Take time on the weekend to finalize your weekly menu, prepare a shopping list, shop, and prep ingredients for the week. Having everything you need at the ready will help you stay on track and avoid the temptations of less-healthy foods. Most of all, be flexible and enjoy trying new recipes and new foods. Aim for progress not perfection, keep portions in check, balance your intake with physical activity, include daily stress management, and be certain to get adequate sleep.

# Week 1

| | Breakfast | Lunch | Dinner |
|---|---|---|---|
| **Monday** | Raspberry Peach Smoothie Bowls | Quinoa Spinach Power Salad | Tofu Kale Scramble |
| **Tuesday** | Roasted Vegetable and Egg Skillet | Chicken and Rice Stew | Lemon Garlic Mackerel |
| **Wednesday** | Carrot Cake Overnight Oats | Thai Chicken Salad | Pocket Eggs with Sesame Sauce |
| **Thursday** | Creamy Millet Porridge with Roasted Berries | Salmon with Mixed Greens and Walnuts | Indian Spiced Cauliflower Fried "Rice" |
| **Friday** | Red Velvet Beet and Cherry Smoothie | Turkish-Style Minted Chickpea Salad | Sesame-Crusted Tuna Steaks |
| **Saturday** | Carrot Cake Overnight Oats | Hearty White Bean and Kale Soup | Loaded Sweet Potatoes |
| **Sunday** | Pumpkin English Muffins | Rustic Vegetable and Bean Soup | Asian Chicken Lettuce Wraps |

## Week 2

| | Breakfast | Lunch | Dinner |
|---|---|---|---|
| **Monday** | Whole-Wheat Blueberry Muffins | Warm Edamame, Green Pea, and Apple Salad | Tofu Vegetable Stir-Fry |
| **Tuesday** | Raspberry Peach Smoothie Bowls | Thai Seafood Soup | Baked Mustard-Lime Chicken |
| **Wednesday** | Banana Nut Muffins | Marinated White Bean Mason Jar Salad | Pork and Asparagus Stir-Fry |
| **Thursday** | Lentil Asparagus Omelet | Creamy Chicken and Chickpea Bean Salad | Rainbow Trout Baked in Foil with Tomatoes and Thyme |
| **Friday** | Apple Cinnamon Quinoa Breakfast Bowl | Spinach Salad with Salmon and Blueberries | Lentil Walnut Burgers |
| **Saturday** | Nutty Blueberry Avocado Smoothie | Chicken Salad with Grapes and Pistachios | Flounder Tacos with Cabbage Slaw |
| **Sunday** | Southwest Sweet Potato Breakfast Hash | Creamy Asparagus Pea Soup | Balsamic Rosemary Chicken |

# Week 3

| | Breakfast | Lunch | Dinner |
|---|---|---|---|
| **Monday** | Eggs in an Avocado | Roasted Garlic and Tomato Lentil Salad | Acorn Squash Stuffed with White Beans and Kale |
| **Tuesday** | Banana Nut Muffins | Chicken Salad with Grapes and Pistachios | Salmon and Summer Squash in Parchment |
| **Wednesday** | Apple Cinnamon Quinoa Breakfast Bowl | Zesty Lime Shrimp and Avocado Salad | Tarragon Sweet Potato and Egg Skillet |
| **Thursday** | Carrot Cake Overnight Oats | Two-Mushroom Barley Soup | Moroccan Spiced Chicken with Sweet Onions |
| **Friday** | Red Velvet Beet and Cherry Smoothie | Halibut Salad with Ginger-Lime Vinaigrette | Edamame Burritos |
| **Saturday** | Roasted Vegetable and Egg Skillet | Sweet Potato and Black Bean Chili | Salmon and Scallop Skewers |
| **Sunday** | Baby Kale Breakfast Salad with Almond Butter Dressing | Slow Cooker Chicken Vegetable Stew | Farro with Sundried Tomatoes, Pine Nuts, and Arugula |

# Week 4

| | Breakfast | Lunch | Dinner |
|---|---|---|---|
| **Monday** | Carrot Cake Overnight Oats | Simple Tomato Basil Soup | Creamy Quinoa, Lentils, and Roasted Root Vegetables |
| **Tuesday** | Whole-Wheat Blueberry Muffins | Salmon with Mixed Greens and Walnuts | Savory Cheesy Rosemary Oatmeal |
| **Wednesday** | Red Velvet Beet and Cherry Smoothie | Curried Vegetable Stew with Quinoa | Pork Medallions with Mustard Sauce |
| **Thursday** | Pumpkin English Muffins | Thai Chicken Salad | Broiled Tuna Steaks with Peppercorn-Lime Rub |
| **Friday** | Eggs in an Avocado | Quinoa Spinach Power Salad | Red Onions Stuffed with Grilled Steak and Spinach |
| **Saturday** | Raspberry Peach Smoothie Bowls | Egg, Carrot, and Kale Salad Bowl | Grilled Chicken Breasts with Plum Salsa |
| **Sunday** | Roasted Vegetable and Egg Skillet | Broccoli and Gold Potato Soup | Salmon and Summer Squash in Parchment |

Raspberry Peach Smoothie Bowls, p. 41

# 3

# Breakfast Bonanza

# Banana Nut Muffins

DAIRY-FREE / PREP TIME: 5 MINUTES / COOK TIME: 30 MINUTES

These giant bakery-worthy banana nut muffins are moist, delicious, and loaded with heart healthy nutrients. Bananas are one of the best sources of dietary potassium, an important mineral involved in blood pressure regulation. Bananas are also high in fiber and a great source of vitamin $B_6$, which helps to break down homocysteine, an amino acid that at high levels is related to a higher risk of cardiovascular disease. Topped with walnuts, rich in omega-3 fatty acid, each muffin provides a serving of whole grains.

Olive oil nonstick cooking spray

⅔ cup sliced very ripe banana

2 teaspoons granulated stevia or 2 tablespoons brown sugar

½ teaspoon baking soda

⅛ teaspoon salt

2 egg whites, beaten

¼ cup unsweetened applesauce

½ teaspoon vanilla extract

½ cup whole-wheat pastry flour

4 tablespoons chopped walnuts

1.  Preheat the oven to 375°F and lightly spray two 7-ounce ramekins with the cooking spray.

2.  In a large bowl, mash the banana with a fork, leaving some lumps for texture. Add the stevia, baking soda, and salt and whisk together for 1 minute.

3.  Add the egg whites, applesauce, and vanilla and stir until combined. Add the flour and stir with a spatula until just combined.

4.  Divide the batter evenly between the ramekins (they should be about half to three-quarters full), then sprinkle the walnuts evenly over the top. Bake for 25 to 30 minutes, or until the tops are golden brown and a toothpick inserted in the center comes out clean.

5.  Let them cool for a few minutes, remove from the ramekins, and serve warm.

*Toss It Together Tip:* Applesauce replaces fats such as butter or oil, which are typically added to baked goods. In addition to using it as a fat replacer, you can stir some into smoothies, mix it into hot cereal, use as a low sugar swap for jelly in a peanut butter and jelly sandwich, or serve alongside chicken or pork.

**Per Serving:** Calories: 322; Fats: 10g; Protein: 11g; Cholesterol: 0mg; Carbohydrates: 49g; Fiber: 4g; Sodium: 394mg

# Whole-Wheat Blueberry Muffins

QUICK & EASY / PREP TIME: 5 MINUTES / COOK TIME: 23 MINUTES

This quick and easy recipe is full of high-fiber whole grains. The fat is replaced by shredded zucchini, which keeps the muffins moist while adding potassium and magnesium and promotes healthy blood pressure. The blueberries provide fiber, potassium, folate, vitamin C, vitamin $B_6$, and phytonutrients, which all support heart health. Filling and delicious, serve these warm for a delectable and healthy breakfast.

Olive oil nonstick cooking spray
¾ cup whole-wheat flour
½ teaspoon baking soda
Pinch salt
2 teaspoons granulated stevia
    or 2 tablespoons
    brown sugar
2 egg whites, beaten
¼ cup shredded zucchini
3 tablespoons nonfat milk
    or plant-based milk
½ teaspoon vanilla extract
½ cup blueberries
    (fresh or frozen)

1. Preheat the oven to 375°F and lightly spray two cups of a giant muffin pan with the cooking spray.

2. In a large bowl, whisk together the flour, baking soda, salt, and stevia. Set it aside.

3. In a small bowl, stir together the egg whites, zucchini, milk, and vanilla.

4. Stir the wet ingredients into the dry ingredients. Gently fold in the blueberries.

5. Divide the batter equally between the prepared muffin cups. Bake for 19 to 23 minutes, or until a toothpick inserted in the center comes out clean.

6. Let them cool for 3 minutes before enjoying.

*Toss It Together Tip:* Blueberries are one of the most nutritious fruits you can eat when it comes to your heart health, due to their high levels of inflammation-reducing antioxidants and phytochemicals. Use leftover berries in smoothies, hot cereals, other baked goods; serve berries with nonfat yogurt, or eat them plain as a healthy snack.

**Per Serving:** Calories: 270; Fats: 1g; Protein: 11g; Cholesterol: 0mg; Carbohydrates: 55g; Fiber: 3g; Sodium: 451mg

# Pumpkin English Muffins

DAIRY-FREE, GLUTEN-FREE, QUICK & EASY / PREP TIME: 1 MINUTE / COOK TIME: 3 TO 4 MINUTES

All you need are a few ingredients and fewer minutes to make these protein- and fiber-rich, dense and filling English muffins. Store-bought breads are surprisingly high in sodium, a nutrient that adds up quickly when following a heart healthy diet. Finding a low-sodium, tasty bread alternative can prove challenging, making this recipe an excellent solution for enjoying bread while adding nutrients to your diet and keeping that sodium in check. Oat flour adds soluble fiber, egg whites provide high-quality protein, and pumpkin adds anti-inflammatory beta-carotene and phytonutrients. These toast up beautifully and have an amazing texture you are sure to love.

Olive oil nonstick cooking spray
½ cup gluten-free oat flour
1 teaspoon baking powder
4 egg whites
¼ cup pumpkin purée
½ teaspoon pumpkin pie spice
½ teaspoon ground cinnamon
Pinch salt
½ to 1 teaspoon granulated
    stevia

1. Spray two 7-ounce ramekins with the cooking spray.

2. In a medium bowl, stir together the oat flour, baking powder, egg whites, pumpkin purée, pumpkin pie spice, cinnamon, salt, and stevia until well combined.

3. Divide the batter evenly between the two ramekins.

4. Place one ramekin in the microwave and microwave on high for 1 minute to 1 minute 30 seconds (depending on your microwave), or until set. Repeat with the second ramekin.

5. Let the muffins cool for a moment, then remove them from the ramekins. Cut each English muffin in half horizontally and toast until done to your liking.

6. Enjoy with nut butter or the spread of your choice.

*Toss It Together Tip:* You can use up ingredients by making several batches of this recipe and freezing the muffins for future use—just slice them before freezing. Leftover pumpkin purée can also be used as a fat replacer in baked goods, as a smoothie ingredient, in hot cereals, in pancakes or waffles, or frozen in ¼- to ½-cup portions for future use.

**Per Serving:** Calories: 157; Fats: 2g; Protein: 11g; Cholesterol: 0mg; Carbohydrates: 25g; Fiber: 4g; Sodium: 149mg

# Raspberry Peach Smoothie Bowls

**GLUTEN-FREE, QUICK & EASY / PREP TIME: 5 MINUTES**

Smoothie bowls are a satisfying and nutritious alternative to cold cereal, and a fresh way to get a variety of essential nutrients. Full of heart healthy nutrients, this recipe gets its creamy base from Greek yogurt, a low-sodium, protein-rich food that is high in blood pressure–regulating potassium and calcium. Sweet and fiber-filled raspberries add antioxidants and phytochemicals as well as potassium, while chia seeds and almonds add a crunch along with essential fats and magnesium, which can reduce cholesterol levels and lower blood pressure. Ready in minutes, this recipe is easy to customize to your personal preferences.

1½ cups plain nonfat
   Greek yogurt
1 cup frozen chopped mango
½ cup frozen banana slices
½ cup frozen raspberries
½ cup unsweetened
   almond milk
1 teaspoon vanilla extract
1 ripe peach, sliced
   (about ⅔ cup)
½ cup fresh raspberries
2 tablespoons sliced almonds
2 tablespoons chia seeds

1. Add the Greek yogurt, mango, banana, raspberries, almond milk, and vanilla to a blender and blend on low until the mixture reaches a soft serve consistency.

2. Scoop into two serving bowls and top each bowl with half the sliced peach, fresh raspberries, almonds, and chia seeds.

3. Enjoy immediately.

*Toss It Together Tip:* Use extra chia seeds as a crispy crumb coating for meat or fish. Simply grind the chia seeds in a coffee grinder until finely powdered, then mix them in with your usual bread crumb coating, or use as a complete substitute, depending on your preference.

**Per Serving:** Calories: 422; Fats: 9g; Protein: 18g; Cholesterol: 0mg; Carbohydrates: 72g; Fiber: 15g; Sodium: 182mg

# Red Velvet Beet and Cherry Smoothie

GLUTEN-FREE, QUICK & EASY / PREP TIME: 5 MINUTES

Sweet and earthy beets are a goldmine of nutrients including nitrates, which the body converts into nitric oxide, a compound that relaxes and dilates blood vessels for improved circulation and lower blood pressure. You might think a smoothie is an odd place to use beets; however, pairing beets with sweet and phytochemical-rich cherries and unsweetened cocoa is a match made in heaven. Full of satiating protein and fiber, this creamy and nutritious smoothie will start your day with almost three servings of fruits and vegetables.

1½ cups plain nonfat
　　Greek yogurt

1 cup unsweetened
　　almond milk

2 tablespoons unsweetened
　　cocoa powder

1 cup frozen cherries

⅔ cup frozen banana slices

½ cup raw peeled and
　　chopped beets

½ cup gluten-free rolled oats

2 pitted Medjool dates

1 teaspoon vanilla extract

1 cup ice cubes

1. Combine all the ingredients in a high-speed blender and blend until smooth.

2. Pour into two tall glasses and serve immediately.

*Toss It Together Tip:* Unsweetened cocoa is rich in flavonoids, an antioxidant that is converted into nitric oxide, which relaxes the blood vessels. Make homemade cocoa, add it to baked goods, top smoothie bowls, stir it into hot cereal, or stir into nonfat or plant-based milk with a dash of stevia for a healthy, low-sugar chocolate milk.

**Per Serving:** Calories: 349; Fats: 4g; Protein: 17g; Cholesterol: 4mg; Carbohydrates: 65g; Fiber: 9g; Sodium: 248mg

# Nutty Blueberry Avocado Smoothie

**QUICK & EASY / PREP TIME: 5 MINUTES**

This creamy, nutty, nutritious smoothie keeps you feeling full throughout the morning. Yogurt is high in protein and rich in calcium. Nutty wheat germ, creamy avocado, and almonds add healthy monounsaturated fats, cholesterol-reducing soluble fiber, and vitamin E. Antioxidant and phytonutrient-rich blueberries provide sweetness, and fresh baby spinach adds nitrates for healthy circulation. With over three servings of fruits and veggies per glass, this smoothie is the perfect way to start your day.

1 cup plain nonfat Greek yogurt

1 cup unsweetened vanilla almond milk

1 teaspoon vanilla extract

2 cups fresh baby spinach

1 cup frozen blueberries

½ cup mashed avocado

¼ cup almonds

2 tablespoons wheat germ

1 teaspoon granulated stevia (or sweetener of choice)

¼ teaspoon ground cinnamon

1 cup ice cubes

1. Combine all the ingredients in a high-speed blender and process until smooth.

2. Pour into two tall glasses and serve immediately.

*Tip:* Make wheat germ a permanent member of your pantry staples. Just 2 tablespoons contain 3 grams of protein and 2 grams of fiber, plus it is a good source of potassium, folic acid, magnesium, B vitamins, vitamin E, and plant sterols. Substitute it for bread crumbs in recipes or filler in meatloaf and meatballs; use as a topping for yogurt and cereals, a nutrition boost for baked goods, or a nutty salad topper; and stir into soups and stews.

**Per Serving:** Calories: 340; Fats: 15g; Protein: 14g; Cholesterol: 2mg; Carbohydrates: 40g; Fiber: 8g; Sodium: 192mg

# Baby Kale Breakfast Salad
# with Almond Butter Dressing

**DAIRY-FREE, GLUTEN-FREE, VEGAN, QUICK & EASY / PREP TIME: 10 MINUTES**

Break out of your breakfast routine and get a jumpstart on your vegetable servings for the day with this energizing breakfast salad. A nutritional powerhouse, kale is high in soluble fiber, which can lower cholesterol levels, a valuable benefit when it comes to cardiovascular support. Artichoke hearts, chickpeas, and hemp seeds add protein, inflammation-reducing omega-3 fats, fiber, vitamins, minerals, and phytochemicals. With a creamy almond butter dressing, together these ingredients pack a flavorful, heart healthy punch.

*For the salad*
4 cups baby kale
1 (7.5 ounce) jar artichoke
    hearts packed in water,
    drained and rinsed, or 3/4
    cup frozen
1 (15-ounce) can chickpeas,
    drained and rinsed
1 cup grape tomatoes, halved
2 tablespoons hemp seeds

*For the dressing*
¼ cup almond butter, unsalted
Juice of 1 lemon
1 tablespoon low-sodium
    soy sauce
1 tablespoon minced garlic
1 tablespoon minced ginger
2 tablespoons water, plus more
    as needed

TO MAKE THE SALAD

1. Wash and dry the baby kale. Set it aside.

2. In a medium bowl, combine the artichoke hearts, chickpeas, tomatoes, and hemp seeds.

TO MAKE THE DRESSING

1. In a small bowl, whisk together all the dressing ingredients, adding additional water as needed to get to the desired consistency.

2. Add the dressing to the artichoke mix and combine until evenly coated.

3. Divide the baby kale between two serving plates. Top with half of the artichoke mixture and serve immediately.

*Tip:* Hemp seeds, also known as hemp hearts, are exceptionally nutritious and rich in healthy fats, protein, and various minerals. They add a protein punch to smoothies and have a creamy texture when blended. Also add to baked goods or hot and cold cereals, blend into homemade dressings, and sprinkle over cooked vegetables.

**Per Serving:** Calories: 500; Fats: 11g; Protein: 26g; Cholesterol: 0mg; Carbohydrates: 46g; Fiber: 24g; Sodium: 523mg

# Southwest Sweet Potato Breakfast Hash

DAIRY-FREE, GLUTEN-FREE, VEGAN / PREP TIME: 10 MINUTES / COOK TIME: 25 MINUTES

Sweet potatoes are naturally sweet and contain numerous nutrients that support heart health including potassium, beta-carotene, vitamin C, vitamin $B_6$, and cholesterol-lowering soluble fiber. Black beans are also filled with fiber, along with high levels of protein. Topped with creamy avocado, which adds healthy fats, fiber, and blood pressure–balancing potassium, this vibrant, balanced dish makes a hearty weekday breakfast or a great weekend brunch.

*For the sweet potato hash*
2 teaspoons olive oil
1 garlic clove, minced
1 cup diced yellow onion
2 cups peeled and cubed
    sweet potatoes
1 cup canned black beans,
    drained and rinsed
½ teaspoon paprika
½ teaspoon ground cumin
Pinch salt
¼ cup chopped fresh cilantro

*For the guacamole*
½ avocado, peeled, seeded,
    and mashed
Juice of ½ lime
Salt

*For the pico de gallo*
½ cup diced grape tomatoes
¼ cup finely diced white onion
¼ cup chopped fresh cilantro
Salt

TO MAKE THE SWEET POTATO HASH

Heat the olive oil in a large skillet over medium heat. Add the garlic, onion, sweet potatoes, black beans, paprika, cumin, and salt. Cook for 20 to 25 minutes, stirring every few minutes until the potatoes become tender and slightly caramelized. Remove from the heat and stir in the fresh cilantro.

TO MAKE THE GUACAMOLE

In a small bowl, stir together the mashed avocado and lime juice. Season with salt and set it aside.

TO MAKE THE PICO DE GALLO

In a small bowl, stir together the tomatoes, onion, and cilantro. Season with salt and set it aside.

TO ASSEMBLE

Spoon the sweet potato hash onto two plates, and top with the pico de gallo and guacamole. Serve immediately.

*Toss It Together Tip:* Extra black beans can be added to salads or simply heated through and served alongside chicken or fish. You could also make a black bean hummus by puréeing 1 to 2 tablespoons of sesame tahini, a dash of lemon juice, and garlic.

**Per Serving:** Calories: 528; Fats: 16g; Protein: 15g; Cholesterol: 0mg; Carbohydrates: 86g; Fiber: 19g; Sodium: 260mg

# Lentil Asparagus Omelet

GLUTEN-FREE, QUICK & EASY / PREP TIME: 5 MINUTES / COOK TIME: 10 MINUTES

This omelet is rich in cholesterol-lowering fiber, B vitamins, and anti-inflammatory phytochemicals. Eggs are a good source of high-quality protein, vitamin D, choline, and disease-fighting nutrients like lutein and zeaxanthin. Despite these facts, you may be concerned about their cholesterol content. In a change from past recommendations, the Dietary Guidelines and American Heart Association do not limit cholesterol or egg intake, as the available evidence indicates that eggs, when consumed as part of an overall healthy eating pattern, do not affect risk factors for heart disease. Filling and delicious, this dish provides several servings of vegetables.

4 eggs, whisked

1 tablespoon dried thyme

¼ cup chopped onion

1 cup chopped asparagus (about ½ pound asparagus)

½ cup canned lentils, drained and rinsed

½ cup chopped grape tomatoes, for garnish

8 avocado slices, for garnish (optional)

1. In a medium bowl, whisk together the eggs and thyme. Set them aside.

2. Heat a small nonstick skillet over medium heat. Add the onion and asparagus and cook for 2 to 3 minutes. Add the lentils and cook for an additional 2 minutes until heated through. Decrease the heat to low to keep warm.

3. Heat a medium nonstick skillet over medium heat. Whisk the eggs once more, then add half of the eggs to the frying pan and cook for 2 to 3 minutes.

4. Spread half of the asparagus-lentil mixture on one half of the eggs. Cook for 1 to 2 minutes more, then fold the egg over the filling and cook for another 1 to 2 minutes. Remove from the pan and place on a serving plate.

5. Repeat with the remaining ingredients to make the second omelet.

6. Garnish with the chopped tomatoes and avocado slices (if using) and serve immediately.

*Toss It Together Tip:* Make a quick and easy lentil soup with the leftover canned lentils. Simply combine chopped leftover vegetables, low-sodium vegetable broth, lentils, and seasonings like thyme and tarragon, and heat until the vegetables are tender.

**Per Serving:** Calories: 242; Fats: 9g; Protein: 19g; Cholesterol: 327mg; Carbohydrates: 22g; Fiber: 10g; Sodium: 129mg

# Eggs in an Avocado

DAIRY-FREE, GLUTEN-FREE, QUICK & EASY / PREP TIME: 10 MINUTES / COOK TIME: 5 MINUTES

For a one-two punch of omega-3 fatty acids in your breakfast, try cooking eggs in an avocado. Beyond the heart healthy fats and high protein content, this low-sugar and fiber-filled breakfast will kick off your day on a healthy high note. A salad topper of chopped tomatoes and chives add the antioxidant vitamin C, the minerals potassium and magnesium, B vitamins, and inflammation-reducing phytochemicals. This recipe steams the eggs in a pan to cut down on preparation time but you could also bake them (see the Tip below).

1 large avocado, halved, pitted, and peeled

Salt

Freshly ground black pepper

1 tablespoon olive oil, divided

2 large eggs

3 or 4 tablespoons water

½ cup halved cherry tomatoes

¼ cup chopped fresh chives

1. Lay the avocado halves on a clean work surface, hollow-side up. Gently press the avocado down to slightly flatten the bottom so it will sit without tipping. (Keep the hollow part of the avocado intact to crack the eggs into later). Season with salt and pepper.

2. Heat ½ tablespoon of olive oil in a high-sided skillet over medium-high heat. Add the avocado halves, hollow-side up. Allow the avocados to sear for 1 minute. Crack an egg into each hollow. Season the eggs with salt and pepper. Pour 3 or 4 tablespoons of water into the bottom of the pan and cover the pan with a lid. Bring the water to a simmer and let the eggs steam for 3 to 5 minutes, or until the egg whites have set and the yolks are firm (or set to your liking).

3. Meanwhile, in a medium bowl, mix together the tomatoes, chives, and remaining ½ tablespoon of olive oil. Season with salt and pepper.

4. Remove the egg-stuffed avocados to two serving plates. Top with the tomato and chive mixture and serve.

*Tip:* To make this recipe in the oven, halve the avocados leaving the skin on, place each avocado half in a ramekin or small baking dish, crack 1 egg into each avocado half, season with salt and pepper, and place on a baking sheet. Bake at 425°F until the egg is cooked through, about 15 minutes.

**Per Serving:** Calories: 346; Fats: 32g; Protein: 9g; Cholesterol: 186mg; Carbohydrates: 11g; Fiber: 7g; Sodium: 156mg

# Roasted Vegetable and Egg Skillet

DAIRY-FREE, GLUTEN-FREE, QUICK & EASY / PREP TIME: 5 MINUTES / COOK TIME: 7 MINUTES

All too often fresh vegetables go to waste before they are eaten. This breakfast skillet recipe makes it simple to prepare a hearty, healthy breakfast in minutes, making use of vegetables that you have on hand. Make this skillet a regular part of your breakfast routine to use up remaining fresh vegetables before your next shopping trip. Aim for a rainbow of colors to ensure a mix of vitamins, minerals, and phytochemicals. Cilantro is used as a garnish in this recipe but you can use your favorite herbs and spices.

1 tablespoon olive oil

3 cups chopped mixed vegetables (such as zucchini, mushrooms, onions, bell pepper)

1 teaspoon garlic powder

Salt

Freshly ground black pepper

4 eggs

¼ cup chopped fresh cilantro

1. Preheat the broiler.

2. Put the olive oil in a broiler-proof skillet or medium baking dish. Add the vegetables and garlic powder. Season with salt and pepper and toss gently to coat.

3. Place the skillet under the broiler on the middle oven rack for about 2 minutes, then stir and cook for about 2 more minutes.

4. Remove the skillet from the oven, crack the eggs over the veggies, and return to under the broiler.

5. Broil until cooked to your liking: for over easy eggs, about 2 to 3 minutes. Watch closely as the eggs will cook quickly.

6. Divide the vegetable and egg mixture between two serving plates, top with the fresh cilantro, and serve immediately.

*Tip:* This dish is hearty and delicious as is; however, if you prefer bread with your skillet, take it to the next level by toasting a slice of whole-grain bread and topping it with smashed avocado and tomato slices for additional phytonutrients, B vitamins, fiber, and heart healthy fats.

**Per Serving:** Calories: 242; Fats: 17g; Protein: 14g; Cholesterol: 327mg; Carbohydrates: 14g; Fiber: 6g; Sodium: 212mg

# Apple Cinnamon Quinoa Breakfast Bowl

DAIRY-FREE, GLUTEN-FREE, VEGAN, QUICK & EASY / PREP TIME: 5 MINUTES / COOK TIME: 20 MINUTES

Breakfast quinoa is just as filling and easy to make as oatmeal. Quinoa is a complete protein, meaning it has all of the amino acid building blocks that your body needs for tissue repair and other important processes. One of the most nutrient-rich foods there is, quinoa provides valuable amounts of heart healthy phytonutrients, omega-3 fatty acids, fiber, minerals, and anti-inflammatory vitamin E. Here, it is topped with chopped apple—another food with high amounts of cholesterol-lowering fiber—and gets a crunchy finish from almonds and hemp seeds.

½ cup uncooked quinoa

1 cup unsweetened vanilla or unflavored almond milk

1 or 2 cinnamon sticks

½ teaspoon ground cinnamon

Pinch salt

*Toppings*

2 tablespoons sliced almonds

1 cup chopped apple

2 tablespoons hemp seeds

Optional sweeteners: stevia, brown sugar, honey

1. Rinse the quinoa thoroughly in a colander and drain.

2. Transfer the quinoa to a small saucepan and add the almond milk, cinnamon sticks, ground cinnamon, and salt. Bring to a high simmer, cover, and decrease the heat to low. Simmer for 15 minutes.

3. Remove the pan from the heat and let the quinoa sit for 5 minutes until the almond milk is absorbed and the quinoa has cooked through.

4. Divide the quinoa between two serving bowls. Add half the almonds, apple, and hemp seeds to each bowl. Add sweetener, if desired, and serve.

*Tip:* For added sweetness, heat the chopped apple in the microwave with a splash of cinnamon and almond milk until soft. Other flavor combinations to try: almond milk, cherries, and cocoa; light coconut milk, pineapple chunks, and toasted macadamia nuts; almond milk, chopped pear, and toasted pecans; and almond milk, banana, and toasted peanuts.

**Per Serving:** Calories: 360; Fats: 13g; Protein: 14g; Cholesterol: 0mg; Carbohydrates: 49g; Fiber: 9g; Sodium: 151mg

# Carrot Cake Overnight Oats

DAIRY-FREE, GLUTEN-FREE, VEGAN / PREP TIME: 5 MINUTES,
PLUS 8 HOURS OR OVERNIGHT CHILLING TIME

Cholesterol-lowering oats, omega-3–rich walnuts, and antioxidant-packed carrots team up in this deliciously creamy recipe. Carrots are so common it's easy to overlook their powerful benefits. They contain valuable amounts of antioxidant nutrients including vitamin C and phytonutrients like beta-carotene, which protects the cardiovascular system from oxidative damage. Raisins add healthy blood pressure–promoting potassium to create a breakfast worth waking up for.

1 cup gluten-free rolled oats

1½ cups unsweetened almond milk

½ cup grated carrots

1 tablespoon maple syrup

½ teaspoon vanilla extract

1 teaspoon ground cinnamon

¼ teaspoon ground ginger

½ cup chopped walnuts

¼ cup raisins

1. In a medium bowl, mix together the oats, almond milk, carrots, maple syrup, vanilla, cinnamon, ginger, walnuts, and raisins.

2. Divide the oat mixture between two 8-ounce Mason jars or other small, lidded containers and chill in the refrigerator for at least 8 hours, or overnight.

3. In the morning, stir and enjoy.

*Toss It Together Tip:* Raisins are packed with fiber, antioxidants, iron, and heart healthy potassium. They sweeten without refined sugar and give texture to recipes. Try tossing them in salads, adding them to hot cereal, mixing them into baked goods, roasting them with cauliflower, or enjoying them as a post-workout snack.

**Per Serving:** Calories: 488; Fats: 23g; Protein: 15g; Cholesterol: 0mg; Carbohydrates: 62g; Fiber: 9g; Sodium: 130mg

# Smashed Peas, Red Onion, Avocado, and Egg on Toast

DAIRY-FREE, QUICK & EASY / PREP TIME: 5 MINUTES

Avocado and toast makes an incredibly tasty, super satisfying breakfast or snack no matter what time of day hunger strikes. The healthy fats and fiber in avocado can help keep cholesterol in check, while the peas add plant-based protein and cardioprotective B vitamins, and the egg adds a punch of vitamin D and high-quality protein. Quick to prepare, nutrient dense, and delicious, this recipe is an ultra simple meal for two.

2 slices whole-grain bread
½ ripe avocado, sliced
¼ cup peas (fresh or frozen and thawed)
Salt
Freshly ground black pepper
½ red onion, thinly sliced
1 hardboiled egg, cut in half
Fresh basil leaves, for garnish

1.  Toast the bread and set it aside.

2.  In a small bowl, mash half the avocado, add the peas, and mash again. Season with salt and pepper.

3.  Spread the avocado-pea mixture on each slice of toast. Top equally with the remaining avocado slices, red onion slices, egg, and basil.

4.  Enjoy immediately.

*Tip:* For a variation, pump up the protein and calcium by adding 1 to 2 tablespoons of Greek yogurt to the mash. Including nonfat and low-fat dairy products in a heart healthy diet has been shown to be beneficial in maintaining a healthy blood pressure and a healthy weight.

**Per Serving:** Calories: 225; Fats: 13g; Protein: 8g; Cholesterol: 82mg; Carbohydrates: 22g; Fiber: 7g; Sodium: 268mg

# Creamy Millet Porridge
# with Roasted Berries

DAIRY-FREE, GLUTEN-FREE, VEGAN / PREP TIME: 5 MINUTES / COOK TIME: 25 MINUTES

With its nutrient mix of B vitamins, soluble fiber, potassium, and magnesium, millet is a whole grain to consider making a regular part of your heart healthy eating plan. Technically a seed, this nutritious gluten-free grain alternative can be prepared as a creamy breakfast porridge, a mashed potato substitute, or like fluffy rice. Millet is an especially good source of plant lignans, which are converted to friendly flora in our intestines and are thought to protect against heart disease. Perfectly creamy and sweet, with added heart healthy fats from sliced almonds, this filling and nutrient-dense breakfast gets a protein boost from fortified milk.

*For the strawberries*

2 cups quartered strawberries

1 tablespoon maple syrup

*For the millet*

1 cup millet

1½ cups almond milk with
   added protein (or soy milk),
   plus more as needed

1½ cups water

¼ cup sliced almonds

TO MAKE THE STRAWBERRIES

1. Preheat the oven to 375°F.

2. Toss the strawberries with the maple syrup. Roast for 15 to 20 minutes, or until the strawberries are soft and juicy.

TO MAKE THE MILLET

1. In a medium skillet over medium heat, add the millet and lightly toast for 3 to 4 minutes until slightly browned and fragrant. Remove from the heat and cool slightly.

2. Add the millet to a coffee grinder or blender and pulse until it is roughly half grain, half flour.

3. In a medium saucepan over medium-low heat, combine the millet, milk, and water and simmer, stirring frequently, for 15 to 20 minutes, or until it reaches a porridge consistency and the grain pieces are soft. If the grains are not soft, add a bit more milk and continue to cook until the grains are tender.

4. Serve with the roasted strawberries, sliced almonds, and additional milk.

*Tip:* Because the jury is still out on the health benefits of cow's milk, milk alternatives offer a spectrum of nutrient profiles, tastes, and textures to support your needs, preferences, and health goals. Most plant-based milks are fortified with levels of calcium and vitamins D and A that exceed those of dairy milk, but check the nutrition facts panel to be certain. The majority of plant-based milks have little to no protein so go for soy- or protein-fortified plant milks if you are looking for a replacement for animal protein.

**Per Serving:** Calories: 561; Fats: 12g; Protein: 16g; Cholesterol: 0mg; Carbohydrates: 98g; Fiber: 13g; Sodium: 112mg

# Apricot Granola with Fresh Fruit

DAIRY-FREE, GLUTEN-FREE, VEGAN, QUICK & EASY / PREP TIME: 5 MINUTES / COOK TIME: 5 MINUTES

Sometimes you just want a bowl of crunchy granola goodness with milk and fruit. Granola is the perfect topping for smoothies, fresh fruit, and yogurt, yet packaged varieties are shockingly high in calories, added fats, salt, and sugar. A serving size for granola is just ¼ cup and most brands pack over 200 calories and added fats into that little serving size. While most home-made granola recipes take over 2 hours to make, this recipe, packed with heart healthy fiber and fats from nuts and flaxseed, can be made in just 10 minutes! And you can customize it with your favorite dried fruit, seeds, and spices.

¼ cup gluten-free rolled oats

2 tablespoons almonds

2 tablespoons walnuts

2 tablespoons ground flaxseed

¾ tablespoon olive oil

1 tablespoon maple syrup

Pinch ground cinnamon

¼ cup chopped dried apricots

1 mango, peeled and chopped

¾ cup fresh strawberries

½ cup fresh blueberries

Nonfat dairy milk or plant-based milk, for topping

1. Add the oats, almonds, walnuts, and flaxseed to a small pan over medium heat.

2. Stir until the oats and nuts are warm and starting to brown, 3 to 4 minutes.

3. Pour the olive oil into the pan and stir until mixed through.

4. Pour the maple syrup into the pan and stir until mixed through.

5. Add the cinnamon and stir, then add the dried apricots and mix until combined.

6. Take off the heat and let it cool.

7. Peel and chop the mango, wash and slice the strawberries, and wash the blueberries.

8. Portion the granola into two serving bowls and top with the fresh fruit and milk.

9. Enjoy immediately.

*Toss It Together Tip:* Use up remaining oats, almonds, walnuts, and ground flaxseed by measuring out the portions needed for the recipe and storing in resealable plastic bags. Having the recipe prepped and at the ready will make it easy to cook this heart healthy breakfast whenever a craving for crunchy granola strikes.

**Per Serving:** Calories: 378; Fats: 17g; Protein: 8g; Cholesterol: 0mg; Carbohydrates: 54g; Fiber: 9g; Sodium: 6mg

# Overnight Chia Seed and Coconut Milk Pudding

DAIRY-FREE, GLUTEN-FREE / PREP TIME: 5 MINUTES, PLUS 8 HOURS OR OVERNIGHT CHILLING TIME

Chia seeds and coconut milk come together for a filling pudding that works great for breakfast. High in anti-inflammatory omega-3 fatty acids, this sweet chia pudding is a make-ahead recipe that will save you time, fill you up with fiber and protein, and add the valuable immune-supporting antioxidant vitamins C and A to your day. With a dusting of phytochemical-rich cocoa, this delicious dish will make you forget all about that donut or processed bowl of cereal.

½ cup chia seeds

2 cups light coconut milk

3 teaspoons honey, divided

¼ cup sliced banana

¼ cup fresh raspberries

½ tablespoon sliced almonds

½ tablespoon chopped walnuts

2 teaspoons unsweetened
     cocoa powder, divided

1. Mix the chia seeds, coconut milk, and 2 teaspoons of honey together in a small bowl. Portion into two glass Mason jars and refrigerate for 8 hours or overnight.

2. Remove the jars from the refrigerator and top each jar with half the banana, raspberries, almonds, walnuts, and cocoa. Drizzle each jar with the remaining 1 teaspoon of honey, dividing it equally.

3. Enjoy immediately.

*Toss It Together Tip:* Use remaining chia seeds, coconut milk, and honey by prepping enough jars for the week and storing them in the refrigerator. Having the jars prepped and ready to go will make it easy to know exactly what to reach for on busy mornings.

**Per Serving:** Calories: 732; Fats: 63g; Protein: 13g; Cholesterol: 0mg; Carbohydrates: 41g; Fiber: 18g; Sodium: 38mg

Quinoa Salad with Chicken and Apple, p. 75

# 4

# Meal-Sized Salads

# Roasted Garlic and Tomato Lentil Salad

DAIRY-FREE, GLUTEN-FREE, VEGAN / PREP TIME: 15 MINUTES / COOK TIME: 30 MINUTES

Whole books have been written about the health benefits of garlic, an herb affectionately called the "stinking rose." A member of the *Allium* family, garlic is rich in a variety of powerful sulfur-containing compounds shown through research to have important cardioprotective properties including its ability to lower triglyceride and cholesterol levels. While raw garlic is too strong for many people, roasted garlic is sweet, mild, and almost syrupy in taste. Coupled with protein and fiber-rich lentils, this elegant salad has an irresistible aroma and delectable taste.

1 whole garlic bulb

1 tablespoon olive oil, plus
  2 teaspoons, divided

1 cup halved grape tomatoes

½ cup sliced red onion

Salt

Freshly ground black pepper

1 cup low-sodium
  vegetable broth

½ cup green lentils

½ cup diced red bell pepper

¼ cup diced celery

¼ cup pumpkin seeds

¼ cup finely chopped
  fresh parsley

1 tablespoon freshly squeezed
  lemon juice

Pinch red pepper flakes

1. Preheat the oven to 375°F and line a baking sheet with parchment paper.

2. Cut the top off the garlic bulb and place it on a small piece of aluminum foil. Drizzle the bulb with 1 teaspoon of olive oil and close the foil around the garlic.

3. Arrange the tomatoes and onion in a single layer on the prepared baking sheet and drizzle with 1 teaspoon of olive oil. Sprinkle with salt and pepper.

4. Bake the wrapped garlic and the vegetables for 25 to 30 minutes, or until slightly shriveled.

5. Meanwhile, in a medium saucepan, bring the broth to a boil. Add the lentils, decrease the heat, cover, and simmer for 20 to 25 minutes, or until tender. Drain and transfer to a bowl.

6. Carefully open the garlic packet and allow the garlic to cool. Gently press the cloves from the bulb into a small bowl and use the back of a fork to break up the garlic into smaller pieces.

7. Add the garlic, baked tomatoes and onion, bell pepper, celery, pumpkin seeds, and parsley to the lentils.

8. In a small bowl, whisk together the remaining 1 tablespoon of olive oil, the lemon juice, and red pepper flakes. Season with salt and pepper. Toss the dressing with the lentil mixture and serve.

*Tip:* Lentils are marketed in four general categories: green, brown, red/yellow, and specialty. In general, brown and green varieties retain their shape well, whereas red and specialty lentils tend to disintegrate when cooked, making them best suited to soups or applications where they will be puréed.

**Per Serving:** Calories: 368; Fats: 21g; Protein: 16g; Cholesterol: 0mg; Carbohydrates: 33g; Fiber: 11g; Sodium: 389mg

# Quinoa Spinach Power Salad

DAIRY-FREE, GLUTEN-FREE, VEGAN, QUICK & EASY / PREP TIME: 5 MINUTES / COOK TIME: 10 MINUTES

This salad is bursting with tomatoes, snap peas, cucumbers, and almonds, and dressed in a lemony vinaigrette. Colorful and refreshing, each ingredient is packed with nutrients, making this a complete meal for two. Gluten-free quinoa stands out from other grains because of its high protein content and array of nutrients including B vitamins, fiber, and other minerals. And quinoa isn't the only power food in this salad. Spinach is loaded with vitamins, minerals, and antioxidants that promote a healthy cardiovascular system. With healthy fats and contrasting crunch from the almonds, this salad is easy to customize by adding in your favorite ingredients.

2 cups water

½ cup uncooked quinoa, rinsed and drained

2 cups finely chopped spinach

1 cup sugar snap peas

¾ cup diced tomato

½ cup diced cucumbers

¼ cup sliced almonds

1½ tablespoons freshly squeezed lemon juice

1½ tablespoons olive oil

¼ teaspoon salt

¼ teaspoon freshly ground black pepper

1. Bring the water to a boil in a medium saucepan. Add the quinoa and continue to boil until the quinoa is tender, about 10 minutes.

2. Drain the quinoa and let it cool.

3. In a large bowl, combine the spinach, peas, tomato, cucumber, almonds, and cooled quinoa.

4. In a small bowl, whisk together the lemon juice, olive oil, salt, and pepper. Drizzle over the salad and toss to coat.

5. Divide between two serving bowls and enjoy.

*Tip:* Rinsing quinoa removes quinoa's natural coating, called saponin, which can make it taste bitter or soapy. Although boxed quinoa is often rinsed, it doesn't hurt to give it a rinse at home. Because the seeds are so tiny and you don't want to lose them down the drain, use a very fine mesh strainer. A standard gold coffee filter works great as well!

**Per Serving:** Calories: 322; Fats: 18g; Protein: 11g; Cholesterol: 0mg; Carbohydrates: 32g; Fiber: 8g; Sodium: 325mg

# Kale Avocado Salad with Roasted Carrots

DAIRY-FREE, GLUTEN-FREE, VEGAN / PREP TIME: 10 MINUTES / COOK TIME: 30 MINUTES

Choosing avocados for your heart healthy eating plan can help you keep your cholesterol and blood pressure in check, and may also be able to help you control your weight. An excellent source of healthy monounsaturated fats, avocados contain high amounts of soluble fiber and are a good source of plant sterols, a type of phytochemical with cholesterol-lowering properties. Baby carrots and omega-3 rich walnuts are roasted to sweet perfection, softening nutritional superstar kale, and tying together this nutritious, satisfying salad.

1 cup baby carrots, halved lengthwise

1 teaspoon olive oil

⅛ teaspoon salt

⅛ teaspoon freshly ground black pepper

½ (15-ounce) can chickpeas, drained and rinsed

2 tablespoons coarsely chopped walnuts

4 cups stemmed and coarsely chopped kale

2 teaspoons freshly squeezed lemon juice

1 large ripe avocado, peeled, pitted, and cubed

1. Preheat the oven to 400°F.

2. In a small bowl, toss together the carrots, olive oil, salt, and pepper. Transfer to a rimmed baking sheet and bake for 20 minutes.

3. Add the chickpeas and walnuts to the baking sheet, stir, and return to the oven.

4. Bake until the carrots are brown and tender, an additional 5 to 10 minutes.

5. Massage the kale with your hands until the kale softens and turns bright green, about 2 minutes.

6. In a large serving bowl, combine the kale, lemon juice, and half the avocado.

7. Add half the carrot mixture to the kale and toss. Top with the remaining carrot mixture and avocado.

8. Divide between two serving bowls and enjoy.

*Toss It Together Tip:* Beans work just about everywhere and if you have any leftover, you're in for a treat! Add them to smoothies (you won't even notice), roast them in the oven for a healthy, crunchy snack, toss them into salads, stir into soups, or freeze them for future use.

**Per Serving:** Calories: 535; Fats: 30g; Protein: 17g; Cholesterol: 0mg; Carbohydrates: 58g; Fiber: 19g; Sodium: 257mg

# Warm Edamame, Green Pea, and Apple Salad

DAIRY-FREE, GLUTEN-FREE, VEGAN, QUICK & EASY / PREP TIME: 10 MINUTES / COOK TIME: 10 MINUTES

The combination of toasted green peas, chewy edamame, crunchy apples, and cashews paired with the creamy avocado-lime dressing is delicious! Just one-half cup of edamame provides 11 grams of protein, 9 grams of fiber, 10 percent of the daily value for two key antioxidant vitamins A and C—and as much iron as a 4-ounce chicken breast. Phytoestrogens, the phyto-chemicals in soy, have also been shown to reduce bad (LDL) cholesterol, as well as promote a healthy blood pressure. Filling and nutritious, this warm salad is full of flavor and is a power lunch that won't leave you hungry.

*For the dressing*
½ large avocado, peeled and pitted
½-inch piece fresh ginger, peeled and chopped
1 shallot
2 tablespoons freshly squeezed lime juice
½ tablespoon apple cider vinegar
2 teaspoons olive oil
3 tablespoons chopped fresh cilantro

*For the salad*
1 cup green peas (fresh or frozen and slightly thawed)
½ tablespoon olive oil
¼ teaspoon salt, plus more for seasoning
¼ teaspoon ground cumin
⅛ teaspoon ground ginger
½ cup cashews
1½ cups cooked shelled edamame
1 cup chopped apples
Freshly ground black pepper
1 tablespoon chopped fresh cilantro, for garnish

TO MAKE THE DRESSING

Put all the dressing ingredients in a high-speed blender and blend until smooth and creamy.

TO MAKE THE SALAD

1.  Heat a medium skillet over high heat. Add the peas and toast, stirring constantly, for 5 to 8 minutes, or until they start to brown. Drizzle the olive oil over the peas. Add the salt, cumin, and ginger. Stir to coat. Add the cashews and stir. Decrease the heat to medium-high and continue to cook for 2 to 3 minutes, or until the cashews begin to lightly brown.

2.  Transfer the pea-cashew mixture to a medium bowl and add the edamame and apples. Season with salt and pepper. Add the dressing and toss to coat.

3.  Garnish with the cilantro and serve warm.

*Tip:* If you aren't familiar with edamame (immature soybeans), you can usually find them in the freezer section with the frozen vegetables. Buy the shelled kind if you can, to save time, otherwise you will have a longer cooking time and an extra step to remove the beans from their pods. Because soy is one of the crops most likely to be genetically modified, try to buy an organic variety.

**Per Serving:** Calories: 774; Fats: 48g; Protein: 36g; Cholesterol: 0mg; Carbohydrates: 64g; Fiber: 19g; Sodium: 412mg

# Marinated White Bean Mason Jar Salads

**DAIRY-FREE, GLUTEN-FREE, VEGAN, QUICK & EASY / PREP TIME: 10 MINUTES**

Canning jars are perfect for packing with salad ingredients for grab-and-go nutritious meals no matter how hectic life gets. This salad uses fiber and protein-rich white beans marinated with herbs and spices, topped with vitamin C–packed peppers and tomatoes. Arugula, also known as salad rocket, serves as the leafy green. A Mediterranean green with a distinct peppery flavor and aroma, some of arugula's heart healthy benefits include high amounts of calcium, vitamins A, C, and K, phytochemicals, and it promotes healthy blood pressure with potassium. To create other Mason jar salad combinations, see the Tip below.

1 small garlic clove, minced

1 teaspoon chopped
    fresh thyme

½ teaspoon paprika

¼ teaspoon dry mustard
    powder

¼ teaspoon salt

⅛ teaspoon freshly ground
    black pepper

1 tablespoon white wine
    vinegar

1 tablespoon olive oil

1 (15-ounce) can cannellini
    beans, drained and rinsed

½ cup chopped red bell pepper

½ cup halved grape tomatoes

4 packed cups arugula

1. In a medium bowl, whisk together the garlic, thyme, paprika, mustard powder, salt, pepper, and vinegar. While whisking, slowly drizzle in the olive oil until it is incorporated. Add the beans and toss to combine.

2. Divide the marinated white bean salad between two 1-quart Mason jars. Top each jar with half the bell pepper, tomatoes, and arugula. Cover with the lids and refrigerate for up to 5 days.

3. To serve, pour the salads into two serving bowls, toss, and enjoy.

*Tip:* Use this general template to create your own Mason jar salads: add the salad dressing first (this is key to prevent sogginess); add heartier vegetables like carrots, cooked potato cubes, chopped zucchini (or zucchini strips); add beans and/or whole grains; add protein like cooked chicken or tofu; add softer vegetables and/or fruits; add seeds; lastly, add greens.

**Per Serving:** Calories: 356; Fats: 8g; Protein: 21g; Cholesterol: 0mg; Carbohydrates: 54g; Fiber: 22g; Sodium: 314mg

# Turkish-Style Minted Chickpea Salad

**DAIRY-FREE, GLUTEN-FREE, VEGAN, QUICK & EASY / PREP TIME: 10 MINUTES**

Fresh and flavorful, this Turkish-style bean salad is dotted with sundried tomatoes and olives, and dressed with a simple tomato-based dressing. Kalamata olives are rich in anti-inflammatory phytochemicals, contain healthy monounsaturated fats, and are high in fiber and iron. The high monounsaturated fat content of olives has been associated with a lower risk of cardiovascular disease due to their favorable impact on cholesterol. However, olives are high in sodium, so it is important to watch portion sizes. Quick to prepare, the combination of fresh herbs and flavorful vegetables makes this salad a great choice for a satisfying, heart healthy lunch.

½ cup roughly chopped fresh flat-leaf parsley

½ cup roughly chopped fresh mint leaves

½ cup drained and chopped oil-packed sundried tomatoes

1 (7.5-ounce) jar water-packed artichoke hearts, drained, rinsed, and chopped

¼ cup pitted and chopped Kalamata olives

¼ cup finely chopped red onion

1½ tablespoons tomato sauce, no salt added

1 tablespoon freshly squeezed lemon juice

½ tablespoon olive oil

½ teaspoon paprika

1 (15-ounce) can chickpeas, drained and rinsed

½ cup finely chopped seedless cucumber

Add all the ingredients to a large bowl and mix until combined. Serve immediately.

*Toss It Together Tip:* Use up remaining olives and tomato sauce by making a simple sauce for cooked grains or beans: Combine the sauce and olives with freshly chopped tomatoes, red onion, and fresh basil in a small saucepan and heat over medium-high heat until you achieve your desired consistency. Season with salt and pepper.

**Per Serving:** Calories: 550; Fats: 12g; Protein: 25g; Cholesterol: 0mg; Carbohydrates: 85g; Fiber: 31g; Sodium: 588mg

# Egg, Carrot, and Kale Salad Bowl

DAIRY-FREE, GLUTEN-FREE / PREP TIME: 10 MINUTES / COOK TIME: 20 MINUTES

Salad bowls are quick to make and adaptable to whatever vegetables are in season or that you have on hand. In this recipe, warm quinoa and a fried egg are topped with crunchy, spicy radish and fennel to provide a nice texture and taste contrast, while a dressing of tahini and lemon brings together the flavors. Fennel's fiber, potassium, folate, vitamin C, vitamin $B_6$, and phyto-nutrient content all support cardiovascular health. Reminiscent of anise, fennel adds a sweetly musky flavor to this nutritious combination of power foods.

½ cup uncooked quinoa, rinsed

1 cup water

1 cup sliced carrots

4 radishes, sliced

½ fennel bulb, sliced very finely

1 medium avocado, pitted, peeled, and cubed

2 cups stemmed and chopped baby kale

2 cups mixed baby lettuce

3 teaspoons olive oil, divided

2 teaspoons freshly squeezed lemon juice

Pinch salt

Pinch freshly ground black pepper

2 tablespoons tahini (sesame paste)

2 eggs

2 teaspoons hemp seeds

1. Add the quinoa and water to a medium saucepan. Bring to a boil, lower the heat to a simmer, and cook for about 15 minutes, or until tender. Transfer to a large mixing bowl and set it aside to cool.

2. Add the carrots, radishes, fennel, avocado, kale, and lettuce to the quinoa. Drizzle with 2 teaspoons of olive oil, the lemon juice, salt, and pepper and toss to combine. Divide the salad between two bowls and drizzle 1 tablespoon of tahini over the salad in each bowl.

3. Heat the remaining 1 teaspoon of olive oil in a large nonstick skillet over medium heat. Crack the eggs into the skillet, increase the heat to medium-high, and fry the eggs until cooked to your liking, about 3 minutes for over-hard.

4. Transfer one egg to each bowl, top each with 1 teaspoon of hemp seed, and serve immediately.

*Toss It Together Tip:* Tahini is a paste made from sesame seeds with a consistency similar to that of peanut butter. An essential ingredient in hummus, tahini can be added to smoothies, whisked with sesame oil and white wine vinegar to make a vinaigrette, added to soups, and used anywhere you would use peanut butter. For the remaining fennel bulb, shred it and use in salads, or chop and add to soups.

**Per Serving:** Calories: 660; Fats: 47g; Protein: 22g; Cholesterol: 164mg; Carbohydrates: 46g; Fiber: 14g; Sodium: 268mg

# Thai Chicken Salad

DAIRY-FREE, GLUTEN-FREE, QUICK & EASY / PREP TIME: 10 MINUTES / COOK TIME: 15 MINUTES

Perfect fuel for a busy afternoon, this Thai chicken salad is rich in color and texture, and packed with flavor. Lean chicken breast provides ample high-quality protein to keep you feeling full, while the mix of vegetables adds valuable fiber, vitamins, minerals, and phytochemicals. For added heart-protective benefits, fresh ginger is used for a spicy kick and for its cholesterol-lowering abilities, and crunchy cashews add good-for-you monounsaturated fats. This recipe can easily be scaled up for a crowd.

1 tablespoon olive oil, plus
    2 teaspoons, divided
½ cup finely chopped
    red onion
1 teaspoon minced garlic
8 ounces boneless, skinless
    chicken breast
2 tablespoons freshly squeezed
    lime juice
1-inch piece fresh ginger,
    peeled and grated
1 teaspoon red pepper flakes
4 cups shredded Napa cabbage
1 cup snow peas
¾ cup grated carrots
½ cup diced red bell pepper
¼ cup chopped scallions
¼ cup chopped fresh basil
¼ cup chopped fresh cilantro
¼ cup chopped cashews

1.  In a large skillet, heat 2 teaspoons of olive oil over medium-high heat. Add the onion and garlic and cook for 2 minutes. Add the chicken and sauté for 10 to 15 minutes, or until browned and the chicken is fully cooked to an internal temperature of 165°F. Set it aside to cool, then shred the chicken.

2.  In a small bowl, whisk together the lime juice, ginger, and red pepper flakes. Slowly whisk in the remaining 1 tablespoon of olive oil until combined.

3.  In a large bowl, combine the cabbage, snow peas, carrots, bell pepper, scallions, basil, cilantro, and shredded chicken. Add the dressing and toss. Divide between two serving bowls, top with the cashews, and serve.

*Tip:* Napa cabbage is packed with many antioxidant plant compounds such as carotenes, lutein, and zeaxanthin. An abundant source of soluble fiber, the compounds in Napa cabbage may help to reduce cholesterol levels. Buy a fresh, crispy, compact cabbage and store as you would other greens in the fridge. Eat raw, use in stir-fries, and add to sandwiches.

**Per Serving:** Calories: 445; Fats: 21g; Protein: 35g; Cholesterol: 65mg; Carbohydrates: 32g; Fiber: 9g; Sodium: 140mg

# Chicken Salad with Grapes and Pistachios

DAIRY-FREE, GLUTEN-FREE / PREP TIME: 20 MINUTES / COOK TIME: 30 MINUTES

The sweet and savory combination of toppings in this salad—grapes, carrots, and pistachios—creates a flavorful and nutritious mix. High-protein lean chicken breast keeps you feeling satisfied. Pistachios add a savory crunch while offering multiple health benefits, including the ability to lower unhealthy cholesterol levels. In addition to good-for-you fats, pistachios also have plant-based compounds that act as antioxidants, including vitamin E, polyphenols, and carotenoids. Put together, this salad is a cholesterol-lowering powerhouse.

Olive oil nonstick spray

1 cup peeled and sliced carrots

½ tablespoon brown sugar

3 teaspoons olive oil, divided

¼ teaspoon salt, plus pinch, divided

¼ teaspoon freshly ground black pepper, plus pinch, divided

1 (6-ounce) boneless, skinless chicken breast, cut crosswise into thin slices

4 tablespoons sliced scallions, divided

1 tablespoon apple cider vinegar

¼ cup thinly sliced shallot

4 cups baby arugula

1 cup halved seedless red grapes

2 tablespoons unsalted shelled chopped pistachios

1. Preheat the oven to 425°F. Coat a 9-by-9-inch baking pan and a rimmed baking sheet with olive oil cooking spray.

2. Place the carrots in the prepared baking pan. Sprinkle with the brown sugar, 1 teaspoon of olive oil, and ⅛ teaspoon each of salt and pepper. Toss to coat well. Roast, stirring several times, for 25 minutes, or until the carrots are tender and lightly golden at the edges.

3. About 5 minutes before the cooking time is up, place the chicken in a mound on the prepared baking sheet. Drizzle with 1 teaspoon of olive oil, and sprinkle with 2 tablespoons of scallions and the remaining ⅛ teaspoon each of salt and pepper. Toss to mix. Arrange in a single layer. Roast, turning once, for 5 to 7 minutes, or until cooked through to an internal temperature of 165°F. Remove the carrots and chicken from the oven and let them cool for a few minutes.

4. Meanwhile, in a large salad bowl, mix together the vinegar, shallot, remaining 1 teaspoon of olive oil, remaining 2 tablespoons of scallions, and a pinch each of salt and pepper. Let it stand for 5 minutes for the flavors to blend.

5. Add the arugula and grapes to the dressing in the large bowl and toss to mix well. Divide between two serving plates. Top each plate with the carrots, chicken and any juices, and sprinkle each with 1 tablespoon of pistachios. Serve warm.

*Tip:* A 1-ounce serving of pistachios has 49 nuts, more nuts per serving than any other snack nut. Naturally cholesterol- and sodium-free, one serving of pistachios has as much potassium as half a large banana (290 mg) and 3 grams of filling fiber. Pistachios make a great pre- or post-workout snack, a tasty topping to cooked grains and beans, and a healthy addition to egg dishes and baked goods.

**Per Serving:** Calories: 263; Fats: 10g; Protein: 22g; Cholesterol: 49mg; Carbohydrates: 22g; Fiber: 3g; Sodium: 420mg

# Creamy Chicken and Chickpea Salad

### GLUTEN-FREE, QUICK & EASY / PREP TIME: 10 MINUTES

This salad is packed with lean protein, the right amount of heart healthy fat, and is loaded with vitamins, minerals, fiber, and anti-inflammatory phytochemicals to fill you up without weighing you down. Antioxidant-rich cucumbers add a fresh taste and crunch to this salad, which uses calcium-rich Greek yogurt for the creamy dressing. Quick to prepare and full of fresh, nutritious ingredients, the combination of crunchy vegetables and tender chicken breast make this a refreshing main dish salad.

1 cup cubed cooked
  chicken breast
1 (7.5 ounce) can chickpeas,
  drained and rinsed
1 cup chopped seeded
  cucumber
¼ cup chopped scallions
2 tablespoons chopped
  fresh mint
1 garlic clove, minced
¼ cup plain nonfat
  Greek yogurt
Pinch salt
2 cups baby spinach leaves
2 tablespoons sliced almonds
1 lemon, cut into wedges
1 medium tomato, cut
  into wedges

1. Combine the chicken, chickpeas, cucumber, scallions, mint, garlic, yogurt, and salt and toss gently.

2. Gently fold in the spinach.

3. Divide the salad between two serving plates, top with the sliced almonds, place the lemon and tomato wedges on the side, and serve.

*Tip:* Greek yogurt is an excellent source of calcium, vitamin D, protein, and beneficial probiotics. Higher in protein and lower in sugar than regular yogurt, the consistency of Greek yogurt makes it a healthier, lower-fat, and lower-calorie alternative to sour cream and cream cheese. Use it as a high-protein base for smoothies or mixed with avocado for guacamole.

**Per Serving:** Calories: 390; Fats: 8g; Protein: 41g; Cholesterol: 67mg; Carbohydrates: 42g; Fiber: 5g; Sodium: 210mg

# Salmon with Mixed Greens and Walnuts

DAIRY-FREE, GLUTEN-FREE, QUICK & EASY / PREP TIME: 15 MINUTES / COOK TIME: 10 MINUTES

Bursting with heart healthy omega-3 fats from the salmon and walnuts, this high-protein, fiber-packed salad is also rich in B vitamins, vitamin D, and the antioxidant mineral selenium. Most studies on fish intake and cardiovascular health report that while benefits start with only one 6-ounce portion per week, the most benefits come with an intake of 2 or 3 servings per week. Interestingly, a 1-ounce serving of walnuts has even more omega-3 fats per serving than salmon!

2 tablespoons chopped walnuts

½ tablespoon olive oil

4 cups mixed baby greens

½ cup halved button mushrooms

¼ cup chopped red onion

1 teaspoon balsamic vinegar

⅛ teaspoon salt

1 (8-ounce) salmon fillet

Olive oil nonstick cooking spray

1. Preheat the broiler.

2. Heat a large skillet over medium heat. Add the walnuts and toast for 1 minute. Remove the walnuts from the skillet and set them aside.

3. Heat the olive oil in the skillet over medium heat. Add the greens and cook gently for up to 1 minute to wilt a little. Transfer the greens to a medium salad bowl. Add the mushrooms, red onion, balsamic vinegar, and salt and toss to coat.

4. Position an oven rack approximately 8 inches from the heat source. Place the salmon skin-side down in a broiler-proof dish. Spray the surface of the fish with olive oil cooking spray. Broil until the fish flakes easily with a fork, 8 to 10 minutes, depending on the thickness.

5. Divide the salmon into two servings and place on top of the greens and vegetables in the salad bowl. Serve warm.

*Tip:* Walnuts are high in omega-3 fat, vitamins, minerals, and antioxidants. Start adding them to hot cereals, tossing them along with fresh herbs onto salads, sprinkling them on pasta, grinding them to make dips and spreads, and simply eating them as a nutritious snack. They are calorie-dense, however, so stick to 1-ounce portions (about ¼ cup).

**Per Serving:** Calories: 253; Fats: 15g; Protein: 25g; Cholesterol: 50mg; Carbohydrates: 6g; Fiber: 2g; Sodium: 205mg

# Spinach Salad with Salmon and Blueberries

DAIRY-FREE, GLUTEN FREE, QUICK & EASY / PREP TIME: 5 MINUTES / COOK TIME: 10 MINUTES

This superfood salad combines the nutritional power of salmon, blueberries, walnuts, avocado, and chia seeds for a sweet and savory dish that will fill you up while nourishing your heart with an impressive array of vitamins, minerals, phytochemicals, and healthy fats. High in vitamin C and fiber, blueberries should be part of your heart healthy diet as they can lower total cholesterol and decrease the risk of heart disease. Quick to prepare, enjoy the fresh and diverse flavors of this delicious salad.

*For the salad*

1 (8-ounce) salmon fillet, halved crosswise
Olive oil nonstick cooking spray
4 cups baby spinach
½ cup diced avocado
1 cup fresh blueberries
½ cup thinly sliced red onion
2 tablespoons walnuts

*For the dressing*

¼ cup olive oil
2 tablespoons apple cider vinegar
½ tablespoon honey
1 tablespoon chia seeds
Pinch salt

TO MAKE THE SALAD

1. Position an oven rack approximately 8 inches from the heat source. Preheat the broiler to high. Place the salmon skin-side down in a broiler-proof dish. Spray the surface of the fish with olive oil cooking spray. Broil until the fish flakes easily with a fork, 8 to 10 minutes, depending on the thickness.

2. In a medium bowl, combine the spinach, avocado, blueberries, onion, and walnuts, and toss well. Divide between two serving plates. Place a piece of salmon on top of each salad serving.

TO MAKE THE DRESSING

In a small bowl, whisk together the olive oil, vinegar, honey, chia seeds, and salt. Drizzle on top of each salad and serve.

*Tip:* Just about every fruit can be combined with chia seeds to create an unprocessed no-sugar-added jam. Since chia seeds turn liquid into a jelly-like matter, all you need to do is mash up your favorite fruit and combine it with the chia seeds: 1 tablespoon of chia seeds to every 1 cup of mashed fruit.

**Per Serving:** Calories: 609; Fats: 46g; Protein: 28g; Cholesterol: 50mg; Carbohydrates: 27g; Fiber: 10g; Sodium: 181mg

# Halibut Salad with Ginger-Lime Vinaigrette

DAIRY-FREE, GLUTEN-FREE, QUICK & EASY / PREP TIME: 5 MINUTES / COOK TIME: 20 MINUTES

Poaching is a moist-heat cooking technique where food is submerged in a liquid and simmered until cooked through. It is an incredibly versatile cooking method and in this recipe it is used to poach omega-3–rich halibut fillets. Lusciously moist and flavorful, the poached fish is then tossed with crunchy celery and cucumber in a lime-ginger vinaigrette and served over baby greens. A nice alternative to tuna salad, this protein- and fiber-packed salad provides over three servings of vegetables per portion.

1 (8-ounce) boneless, skinless halibut fillet

1 cup water

Zest and juice of 1 lime

1 tablespoon peeled and grated fresh ginger

¼ teaspoon salt

¼ teaspoon freshly ground black pepper

1 cup thinly sliced celery

½ cup peeled, seeded, and diced cucumber

¼ cup chopped fresh parsley

¼ cup thinly sliced scallions

4 cups mixed baby greens

1. Put the halibut in a deep skillet or pot large enough to hold it with only a small amount of space around it. Pour in the water to just submerge the fish. Place the skillet over medium-low heat and cook until the halibut is barely opaque in the center, about 20 minutes. Transfer the fish to a plate to cool. Reserve 1 tablespoon of the poaching liquid and discard the rest.

2. In a large bowl, whisk together the lime zest and lime juice, ginger, salt, pepper, and the reserved 1 tablespoon of poaching liquid.

3. Add the celery, cucumber, parsley, and scallions and toss well. Flake the fish into large pieces, add to the bowl, and toss again.

4. Divide the baby greens between two serving plates. Place half of the halibut mixture on top of each mound of greens and serve.

*Tip:* You can vary the liquid used for poaching, depending on your taste preferences. Other good options are wine, nonfat milk or plant-based milk, and low-sodium vegetable or chicken broth. You can also add herbs and spices to the poaching liquid and an acidic ingredient such as lemon, lime juice, or vinegar to enhance the flavor even further.

**Per Serving:** Calories: 163; Fats: 4g; Protein: 25g; Cholesterol: 36mg; Carbohydrates: 9g; Fiber: 3g; Sodium: 405mg

# Zesty Lime Shrimp and Avocado Salad

DAIRY-FREE, GLUTEN-FREE, QUICK & EASY / PREP TIME: 10 MINUTES

Light, refreshing, healthful, and delicious, this salad requires no cooking and takes just minutes to throw together. Made with cooked and peeled high-protein, low-calorie shrimp, avocado, tomato, red onion, cilantro, and fresh oregano, the salad is gently tossed with freshly squeezed lime juice and a touch of olive oil. While we don't often think of animal protein as a source of antioxidants, shrimp contains two types shown to reduce inflammation in the body.

¼ cup chopped red onion

Juice of 1 lime

1 teaspoon olive oil

⅛ teaspoon salt

⅛ teaspoon freshly ground black pepper

½ pound cooked, peeled, and chopped jumbo shrimp

1 medium tomato, diced

½ large avocado, diced

1 tablespoon chopped fresh cilantro

1 tablespoon chopped fresh oregano

4 cups romaine leaves, chopped

1. In a small bowl, combine the red onion, lime juice, olive oil, salt, and pepper. Let it marinate for at least 5 minutes for the flavors to combine.

2. In a large bowl, combine the shrimp, tomato, and avocado and toss gently. Add the cilantro and oregano and toss gently again.

3. Divide the romaine lettuce between two serving bowls and spoon half of the shrimp mixture over the top of each mound and drizzle with half of the dressing. Serve immediately.

*Toss It Together Tip:* Avocado makes a healthy and delicious replacement for butter on bread. It also lends a creamy consistency to smoothies and works well in just about any salad for added soluble fiber, healthy fats, vitamins, and minerals. Evidence has shown that including avocados at meals boosts satiety.

**Per Serving:** Calories: 283; Fats: 15g; Protein: 28g; Cholesterol: 239mg; Carbohydrates: 12g; Fiber: 5g; Sodium: 433mg

# Quinoa Salad with Chicken and Apple

GLUTEN-FREE, DAIRY-FREE / PREP TIME: 20 MINUTES / COOK TIME: 20 MINUTES

This simple but nutritious salad is full of high-quality protein, fiber, and beneficial phytochemicals. Apples contain a type of fiber called pectin, known to reduce blood cholesterol. They are also rich in vitamin C and catechin polyphenols, antioxidants that decrease oxidation of cell membrane fats, which is especially beneficial for preventing cardiovascular disease. Delicious and easy to prepare, this salad is full of heart healthy benefits.

Olive oil nonstick
   cooking spray
6 ounces boneless, skinless
   chicken breast
⅛ teaspoon salt
½ teaspoon freshly ground
   black pepper
1 cup water
½ cup quinoa, rinsed
¼ cup chopped fresh mint
½ tablespoon olive oil
2 tablespoons red wine vinegar
1 teaspoon Dijon mustard
1 cup diced unpeeled apple
1 small yellow bell pepper, diced
1 Persian cucumber, chopped
2 cups baby spinach
1 tablespoon freshly squeezed
   lemon juice

1. Coat a grill pan with cooking spray and heat over medium-high heat. Season the chicken with the salt and pepper and cook for 8 to 10 minutes per side until it is cooked through and an instant-read thermometer registers 165°F. Cool for 2 to 3 minutes, then cut it into thin strips.

2. Meanwhile, fill a saucepan with the water and add the quinoa. Bring to a boil, reduce the heat to medium low, cover, and simmer for 15 minutes. Fluff the quinoa with a fork and set it aside.

3. In a medium bowl, whisk together the mint, olive oil, vinegar, and mustard. Mix in the apple, pepper, and cucumber. Add the spinach, quinoa, and chicken and toss to coat. Drizzle with the lemon juice.

4. Serve immediately.

*Tip:* The peel of the apples contains many more times the nutrients and insoluble fiber than the flesh, so to reap the most health benefits, leave the peel on. The peel also contains high levels of quercetin, a powerful antioxidant that protects against degenerative diseases. Apples tend to have high residue, so purchase organically grown varieties if possible.

**Per Serving:** Calories: 404; Fats: 8g; Protein: 29g; Cholesterol: 49mg; Carbohydrates: 57g; Fiber: 9g; Sodium: 268mg

Rustic Vegetable and Bean Soup, p. 90

# 5

# Soups & Stews

# Two-Mushroom Barley Soup

DAIRY-FREE, GLUTEN-FREE, VEGAN / PREP TIME: 10 MINUTES / COOK TIME: 25 MINUTES

Two types of mushrooms add rich, deep flavor to this satisfying soup. Mushrooms are one of the very few plant sources of vitamin D, a vitamin that many people have a hard time getting enough of. Shiitake mushrooms also have cardiovascular benefits including cholesterol reduction and immune support due to their unusual mix of phytonutrient antioxidants. If you are cholesterol-conscious, then this soup is for you.

2 teaspoons olive oil

1 cup sliced carrots

1 cup diced onion

½ cup chopped celery

4 cups chopped button
　　mushrooms

1 cup chopped shiitake
　　mushrooms

2 garlic cloves, crushed

1½ teaspoons chopped
　　fresh thyme

⅛ teaspoon salt

⅛ teaspoon freshly ground
　　black pepper

2 cups nonfat milk or
　　plant-based milk

1 cup water

⅓ cup quick-cooking barley

1. Heat the olive oil in a large saucepan over medium heat. Add the carrots, onion, celery, button and shiitake mushrooms, garlic, thyme, salt, and pepper. Cook, stirring, for about 3 minutes, or until the vegetables release some of their juices. Increase the heat to medium-high and continue to cook, stirring often, for another 3 minutes, or until most of the liquid has evaporated.

2. Add the milk, water, and barley. Bring the mixture to a boil, stirring often. Decrease the heat and simmer, stirring occasionally, for about 15 minutes, or until the vegetables and barley are tender.

3. Ladle into bowls and enjoy immediately.

*Tip:* There are more ways than soup to enjoy barley: A bowl of cooked barley with fruit and nuts makes a great change of pace from oatmeal, use barley anywhere you would use rice, grind into flour and use in muffins and quick breads, or use to make risotto.

**Per Serving:** Calories: 331; Fats: 6g; Protein: 18g; Cholesterol: 5mg; Carbohydrates: 54g; Fiber: 10g; Sodium: 384mg

# Hearty White Bean and Kale Soup

DAIRY-FREE, GLUTEN-FREE, VEGAN, QUICK & EASY / PREP TIME: 10 MINUTES / COOK TIME: 20 MINUTES

This simple yet hearty soup combines several heart healthy superfoods in a balanced meal. White beans are cooked in a garlicky rosemary broth with kale for a soup high in fiber, B vitamins, minerals, and inflammation-reducing phytochemicals. A member of the cruciferous vegetable family, kale is one of the most nutritious foods, especially for heart health. It is very high in the flavonoids quercetin and kaempferol, substances that have a positive effect on blood pressure.

1 tablespoon olive oil

1 cup finely sliced onion

½ cup diced red bell pepper

¼ cup diced celery

4 garlic cloves, thinly sliced

1 tablespoon chopped fresh
rosemary leaves

3 cups low-sodium
vegetable broth

1 bay leaf

1 (15-ounce) can white beans,
drained and rinsed

2 cups packed, stemmed, and
finely chopped kale

Salt

Freshly ground black pepper

2 teaspoons freshly squeezed
lemon juice

1. Heat the olive oil in a medium saucepan over medium-high heat. Add the onion, bell pepper, celery, garlic, and rosemary. Cook, stirring often, for about 4 minutes, or until the onions and garlic have softened but not browned.

2. Add the broth, bay leaf, and beans. Bring to a boil, reduce to a slow simmer, and cook for 10 minutes.

3. Add the kale and continue to cook for about 5 minutes until it is completely wilted.

4. Season with salt and pepper. Stir in the lemon juice and serve immediately.

*Tip:* For a heartier soup, add ¼ cup uncooked rinsed quinoa to the soup when the broth is added. Quinoa only takes about 15 minutes to cook and will add additional protein, fiber, vitamins, and minerals to each portion. Quick-cooking barley would also make a great addition to this soup.

**Per Serving:** Calories: 531; Fats: 10g; Protein: 34g; Cholesterol: 0mg; Carbohydrates: 79g; Fiber: 18g; Sodium: 393mg

# Simple Tomato Basil Soup

DAIRY-FREE, GLUTEN-FREE, VEGAN, QUICK & EASY / PREP TIME: 5 MINUTES / COOK TIME: 10 MINUTES

Made with fresh, juicy tomatoes and aromatic fresh herbs, this vibrant soup takes only ten minutes to make. A classic, this recipe tastes best using fresh seasonal produce. Tomatoes are an excellent source of the phytonutrient lycopene, which protects our cells from destructive free radicals. Cooking tomatoes in a healthy fat like olive oil helps carry the lycopene into the bloodstream so the body can get the most benefit from it. Tomatoes are also an excellent source of vitamins C and A, potassium, and fiber. Serve this soup with some crusty whole-grain or sourdough bread.

1 teaspoon olive oil

1 cup chopped onion

4 garlic cloves, minced

7 cups chopped fresh tomatoes (aim for a mix of large, cherry, grape, and heirloom)

½ cup chopped fresh basil leaves

⅛ teaspoon salt

1 teaspoon freshly ground black pepper

1. Heat the olive oil in a medium saucepan over medium heat. Add the onion and garlic and cook for 1 to 2 minutes.

2. Add the tomatoes and continue to cook, stirring every few minutes until the tomatoes have broken down and are soft.

3. Remove from the heat and add the basil, salt, and pepper.

4. Purée in a blender or use an immersion blender until smooth. Serve immediately.

*Tip:* Instead of pairing this soup with the typical grilled cheese sandwich, which is high in unhealthy saturated fat and cholesterol, make a healthier version by skipping the butter and replacing it with avocado, and using a smaller portion of a stronger flavored cheese such as extra-sharp Cheddar.

**Per Serving:** Calories: 169; Fats: 4g; Protein: 7g; Cholesterol: 0mg; Carbohydrates: 33g; Fiber: 9g; Sodium: 182mg

# Broccoli and Gold Potato Soup

DAIRY-FREE, GLUTEN-FREE, VEGAN / PREP TIME: 10 MINUTES / COOK TIME: 35 MINUTES

Here's another reason to eat your broccoli: It may help your heart. A member of the *Brassica* genus, broccoli is known as a cruciferous vegetable and, like others in this group (cabbage, kale, Brussels sprouts), broccoli offers a wealth of health benefits. One of the anti-inflammatory phytochemicals in broccoli, sulforaphane, may decrease the risk of heart attacks and strokes. The fiber in broccoli provides cholesterol-lowering benefits, especially when this nutritious vegetable is cooked. Enjoy this thick and creamy broccoli-potato soup knowing you are reaping heart healthy benefits.

1 tablespoon olive oil

½ cup diced onion

1 garlic clove, minced

3 cups low-sodium vegetable broth

2 cups peeled and chopped Yukon gold potatoes

2 cups broccoli florets

¼ teaspoon dried thyme

¼ teaspoon red pepper flakes

Salt

Freshly ground black pepper

¼ cup chopped fresh chives, for garnish

1. Heat the olive oil in a large saucepan over medium heat. Add the onion and garlic and cook 4 or 5 minutes until fragrant and translucent.

2. Add the vegetable broth and potatoes. Cover and bring to a boil. Decrease the heat to medium and cook for about 15 minutes, or until the potatoes are tender.

3. Add the broccoli, thyme, and red pepper flakes, cover, and steam for 5 minutes, or until the broccoli is cooked but still bright green.

4. Purée the soup in a blender or with an immersion blender. Season with salt and pepper.

5. Ladle into bowls, garnish with the chives, and serve.

*Tip:* For more health benefits, leave the skins on the potatoes. Ounce for ounce, potato skin has far more fiber, iron, potassium, and B vitamins than the flesh. It's also rich in antioxidants. The only reason to avoid the skin is if the potato has a greenish tinge.

**Per Serving:** Calories: 268; Fats: 10g; Protein: 13g; Cholesterol: 0mg; Carbohydrates: 35g; Fiber: 7g; Sodium: 587mg

# Creamy Asparagus Pea Soup

### DAIRY-FREE / PREP TIME: 5 MINUTES / COOK TIME: 25 MINUTES

This simple, heart healthy creamy soup is as tasty as it is nutritious. Asparagus is high in the amino acid arginine, a natural diuretic, which is especially beneficial to people with high blood pressure. Soy milk lends the soup its creaminess without the cholesterol or saturated fat typically found in dairy milk, while adding protein and phytonutrient isoflavones for cardio-vascular support. Shallots and garlic add fiber and inflammation- and cholesterol-lowering phytochemicals. Homemade whole-grain croutons add the finishing touch.

*For the soup*

12 ounces (1 large bundle) asparagus, trimmed

2 teaspoons olive oil, plus more for drizzling

Salt

Freshly ground black pepper

2 garlic cloves, minced

⅓ cup thinly sliced shallots

1 cup fresh or frozen peas

1½ cups plain soy milk

1½ cups low-sodium vegetable broth

*For the garlic herb croutons*

1 cup cubed whole-grain bread

1 tablespoon olive oil

⅛ teaspoon garlic powder

⅛ teaspoon freshly ground black pepper

⅛ teaspoon dried oregano

⅛ teaspoon dried basil

Grated Parmesan cheese, for garnish (optional)

TO MAKE THE SOUP

1. Preheat the oven to 400°F.

2. Spread the asparagus on a baking sheet. Drizzle with olive oil and season lightly with salt and pepper. Toss to coat.

3. Roast for 15 minutes, then set it aside. Lower the oven temperature to 325°F.

4. Heat 2 teaspoons of olive oil in a large saucepan over medium heat. Add the garlic and shallots and cook for 2 to 3 minutes, or until fragrant and translucent.

5. Add the peas, soy milk, and vegetable broth and season with salt and pepper. Bring to a boil, lower the heat, and simmer for 5 minutes.

6. Transfer the roasted asparagus and soup to a blender and blend until creamy and smooth. Transfer the soup back to the pot and simmer over medium heat.

**TO MAKE THE GARLIC HERB CROUTONS**

1.  Add the bread cubes to a large mixing bowl. In a small bowl, whisk together the olive oil, garlic powder, pepper, oregano, and basil and pour over the bread cubes. Toss to coat.

2.  Spread the bread cubes on a clean baking sheet and bake for 15 to 20 minutes, or until golden brown. Stir at the 10-minute mark to ensure even baking.

3.  Ladle the soup into bowls, top with croutons, a touch of black pepper, Parmesan cheese (if using), and serve.

*Tip:* The most common asparagus is green, but you might see others in the store: white, which is more delicate and difficult to harvest, and purple, which is smaller and fruitier in flavor. No matter the type you choose, asparagus is a tasty vegetable that can be enjoyed in a myriad of ways.

**Per Serving:** Calories: 393; Fats: 17g; Protein: 20g; Cholesterol: 0mg; Carbohydrates: 44g; Fiber: 9g; Sodium: 543mg

# Thai Seafood Soup

DAIRY-FREE / PREP TIME: 20 MINUTES / COOK TIME: 20 MINUTES

This Thai-inspired soup is made with high-protein scallops and cod, both excellent sources of omega-3 fats, which can help reduce your risk of heart disease by lowering triglyceride levels. Cod is also a rich source of vitamins $B_{12}$ and $B_6$—both are needed to keep homocysteine levels low—and a very good source of niacin, another B vitamin important for keeping cholesterol in check. Flavored with fresh lemongrass, this simple and satisfying soup is a great way to boost your weekly intake of omega-3 fats.

½ tablespoon olive oil

2 garlic cloves, minced

1 cup sliced button mushrooms

1 cup julienned red bell pepper

2 cups low-sodium chicken broth

¼ pound sea scallops, halved

¼ cup thin diagonally sliced scallions

½ cup grated carrots

2 (2-inch) lengths lemongrass from bottom of stalk, smashed

6 ounces cod or haddock fillet, cut into 2-inch chunks

Zest of 1 lime

¼ cup fresh cilantro leaves

1 teaspoon peeled and grated fresh ginger

1 teaspoon reduced-sodium soy sauce

½ teaspoon red pepper flakes

1. Heat the olive oil in a large saucepan over medium heat. Add the garlic and sauté for 1 to 2 minutes. Add the mushrooms and sauté for 2 minutes. Add the bell pepper and sauté for 2 to 3 minutes, until softened.

2. Add the chicken broth, scallops, scallions, carrots, and lemongrass, and gently simmer for 5 minutes. Add the cod and lime zest and simmer for 5 minutes longer.

3. Stir in the cilantro, ginger, soy sauce, and red pepper flakes. Remove and discard the lemongrass before serving.

*Tip:* A healthy gluten-free alternative to traditional soy sauce is Bragg's liquid aminos. No table salt or preservatives are added and it is certified non-GMO. It contains essential and non-essential amino acids, is alcohol-free, unfermented, and wheat-free. The taste is very similar to soy sauce but the sodium content is much lower.

**Per Serving:** Calories: 256; Fats: 6g; Protein: 36g; Cholesterol: 65mg; Carbohydrates: 13g; Fiber: 2g; Sodium: 397mg

# Slow Cooker Chicken Vegetable Stew

**DAIRY-FREE / PREP TIME: 10 MINUTES / COOK TIME: 4 HOURS**

When cooking for two, a small slow cooker is a wonderful kitchen appliance to consider adding to your equipment repertoire; you just add your ingredients, turn it on, and walk away. This recipe is simple but delicious; one you will want to make time and again. Full of high-quality lean protein and lots of vitamin- and mineral-rich veggies, this fiber-filled soup will keep you energized and hydrated.

1 skinless, boneless chicken breast, trimmed and cut into ½-inch cubes
1 cup cauliflower florets
¾ cup sliced carrots
½ cup halved button mushrooms
½ cup chopped onion
¼ cup diced celery
2 garlic cloves, minced
2 cups low-sodium chicken broth
1 bay leaf
¼ teaspoon freshly ground black pepper

1. Add the chicken, cauliflower, carrots, mushrooms, onion, celery, and garlic to the insert of a 3.5-quart slow cooker. Add the chicken broth, bay leaf, and pepper. Add some water if the mixture looks too thick.

2. Cook on the low heat setting for 4 hours.

3. Ladle into bowls and serve.

*Tip:* You could easily add a grain like brown or wild rice, farro, barley, millet, or buckwheat. Simply add ¼ cup of your chosen grain at the 2-hour mark. You may need to add more water if the soup looks too thick.

**Per Serving:** Calories: 257; Fats: 8g; Protein: 32g; Cholesterol: 75mg; Carbohydrates: 12g; Fiber: 3g; Sodium: 356mg

# Garden Vegetable Stew with Toasted Cashews

DAIRY-FREE, GLUTEN-FREE, VEGAN / PREP TIME: 10 MINUTES / COOK TIME: 30 MINUTES

This stew glows with abundant fresh garden vegetables. Eating seasonally and buying locally grown produce is one of the best ways to obtain peak nutrition from your vegetables. Because the vegetables don't travel very far, they retain more of their nutrients than the produce stocked in most grocery stores. The flavor base for this recipe relies on the cayenne pepper, onions, garlic, and tamari, so you can change up the vegetables based on the season and what you have on hand. Serve this stew with some crusty whole-grain bread.

1 tablespoon olive oil, plus
    2 teaspoons, divided
1 small cayenne pepper,
    seeded and minced
½ cup chopped onion
½ cup chopped red bell pepper
2 garlic cloves, minced
2 teaspoons low-sodium
    tamari sauce
2 cups water
½ cup thinly sliced carrots
½ cup diced fresh tomato
1 cup chopped eggplant
1 cup sliced green beans
¾ cup fresh corn kernels
½ cup raw cashews
½ cup thinly sliced shallots
2 cups chopped Swiss chard
Salt
Freshly ground black pepper

1. Heat 1 tablespoon of olive oil in a large saucepan over medium heat. Add the cayenne pepper, onion, bell pepper, and garlic and cook for about 2 minutes, or until very fragrant and the onion has softened slightly.

2. Add the tamari and water. Bring to a boil, then add the carrots. Decrease the heat and simmer for 3 minutes.

3. Add the tomato and eggplant and cook for 1 minute. Add the green beans and corn and cook for 2 to 3 more minutes. Decrease the heat to low.

4. Meanwhile, in a small sauté pan, heat 1 teaspoon of olive oil over medium-low heat. Add the cashews to the pan and toast them for 4 to 5 minutes, or until they brown on all sides. Transfer them to a small plate.

5.  Return the sauté pan to the heat and add the remaining 1 teaspoon of olive oil. Add the shallots to the pan and stir for 10 to 15 minutes, or until they turn a deep brown and crisp in some areas. Set them aside.

6.  Bring the pot of stew back to a boil and add the Swiss chard. Cook until the greens wilt, about 1 minute. Season with salt and pepper.

7.  Ladle the stew into serving bowls, top each bowl with toasted cashews and some shallots, and serve.

*Tip:* To increase protein, add chicken, diced tofu, or a can of beans. For chicken, choose a skinless breast, dice it, and add it in step 3 with the tomato and eggplant. You could also cook it separately in a sauté pan and add it during the last minutes of simmering.

**Per Serving:** Calories: 457; Fats: 29g; Protein: 12g; Cholesterol: 0mg; Carbohydrates: 47g; Fiber: 9g; Sodium: 500mg

# Sweet Potato and Black Bean Chili

DAIRY-FREE, GLUTEN-FREE, VEGAN, QUICK & EASY / PREP TIME: 5 MINUTES / COOK TIME: 20 MINUTES

This satisfying vegan chili is studded with fiber- and protein-loaded black beans and beta-carotene–rich sweet potatoes. Both the USDA Food Pattern and the Dietary Approaches to Stop Hypertension (DASH) Eating Plan recommend including at least 4 to 5 cups of beans per week to promote heart health. They are recommended because of what they contain (fiber and potassium) as well as what they don't contain (no saturated fat, trans fat, cholesterol, or sodium). Savory, sweet, and spicy, this chili, served with a green salad and orange slices, would make a perfect Meatless Monday meal.

2 teaspoons olive oil

1 cup peeled and diced
    sweet potato

½ cup finely sliced onion

½ cup diced red bell pepper

2 garlic cloves, minced

1 tablespoon chili powder

2 teaspoons ground cumin

1 teaspoon smoked paprika

⅛ teaspoon salt

1⅓ cups water

1 (15-ounce) can black beans,
    drained and rinsed

1 cup diced tomatoes,
    with juice

2 teaspoons freshly squeezed
    lime juice

2 tablespoons chopped
    fresh cilantro

1. Heat the olive oil in a large saucepan over medium-high heat. Add the sweet potato, onion, and bell pepper and cook for about 4 minutes, stirring often, or until the onion has slightly softened.

2. Add the garlic, chili powder, cumin, paprika, and salt and cook for about 30 seconds, stirring constantly, or until fragrant. Add the water and simmer, covered, for 10 to 12 minutes, until the sweet potato is tender.

3. Add the beans, tomatoes and their juices, and lime juice and return to a simmer, stirring often. Decrease the heat and simmer for about 4 minutes, or until slightly reduced.

4. Remove from the heat, stir in the cilantro, and serve.

*Tip:* To make a black bean hummus, in a food processor combine a can of rinsed, drained black beans with 1 tablespoon of sesame tahini, garlic, fresh parsley, black pepper, and olive oil and process until smooth and creamy.

**Per Serving:** Calories: 475; Fats: 7g; Protein: 24g; Cholesterol: 0mg; Carbohydrates: 84g; Fiber: 25g; Sodium: 234mg

# Curried Vegetable Stew with Quinoa

**DAIRY-FREE, GLUTEN-FREE, VEGAN / PREP TIME: 10 MINUTES / COOK TIME: 25 MINUTES**

This flavorful, aromatic vegetable stew is like a big bowl of warm comfort. It's chockfull of nutrients including complete protein from the quinoa, heart healthy fiber and potassium from the beans, and antioxidant vitamins including vitamins A and C from the bell peppers and carrots. With a touch of richness and healthy fats from the peanut butter, this stew may become your go-to weeknight dinner. Vary the vegetables to your liking and serve with some crusty whole-grain bread.

½ tablespoon olive oil

½ cup chopped red onion

½ cup chopped green
   bell pepper

½ cup chopped red bell pepper

½ cup chopped carrots

¼ cup chopped celery

2 garlic cloves, minced

1 tablespoon peeled and
   minced fresh ginger

½ tablespoon curry powder

1 cup peeled, seeded, and
   chopped tomato

1 bay leaf

2 cups low-sodium
   vegetable broth

½ cup quinoa, rinsed

1 (15-ounce) can red beans,
   drained and rinsed

1 tablespoon natural peanut
   or almond butter

2 tablespoons raisins

¼ cup chopped fresh cilantro

6 cups fresh baby spinach
   leaves, torn into
   bite-size pieces

Salt

Freshly ground black pepper

1. Heat the olive oil in a 4-quart saucepan or Dutch oven over medium heat. Add the onion, green and red bell peppers, carrots, and celery, and sauté for about 5 minutes, or until the vegetables are soft and translucent.

2. Add the garlic, ginger, and curry powder, and sauté until fragrant, about 2 minutes. Add the tomato and bay leaf and cook, uncovered, for about 3 minutes, or until the tomato juices have slightly reduced.

3. Add the broth and bring the mixture to a boil. Decrease the heat to low and add the quinoa. Simmer for about 12 minutes. Stir in the beans and peanut butter until the peanut butter melts. Cook for about 2 minutes, or until heated through. Stir in the raisins, cilantro, and spinach. Season with salt and pepper and serve immediately.

*Tip:* Kale would also work well in this recipe in place of the spinach. Another option would be to add cubed eggplant. Eggplant is one of those incredibly versatile vegetables and its dense, meaty texture would make a nice complement to the firmer vegetables in this recipe.

**Per Serving:** Calories: 644; Fats: 14g; Protein: 36g; Cholesterol: 0mg; Carbohydrates: 103g; Fiber: 23g; Sodium: 434mg

# Rustic Vegetable and Bean Soup

DAIRY-FREE, GLUTEN-FREE, VEGAN / PREP TIME: 10 MINUTES / COOK TIME: 35 MINUTES

Endlessly variable, vegetable and bean soups are a winning combination that delivers delicious nourishment to please almost any palate. The gentle, earthy character of protein- and fiber-rich navy beans makes them a perfect backdrop for the sweet, aromatic flavor of marjoram, a popular Mediterranean herb high in phytochemicals and vitamins A, C, and K. The phytochemicals in the garlic and shallots help reduce cholesterol, and this hearty soup provides several servings of vegetables in each portion.

1 tablespoon olive oil

½ cup chopped celery

½ cup chopped shallots

Salt

Freshly ground black pepper

2 garlic cloves, minced

1 tablespoon chopped
    fresh marjoram

½ cup chopped carrots

½ cup peeled and diced
    gold potatoes

½ cup chopped tomatoes,
    with juices reserved

3 cups low-sodium vegetable
    broth, divided

1 (15-ounce) can navy beans,
    drained and rinsed

2 teaspoons red wine vinegar

¼ cup thinly sliced chives,
    for garnish

1. Heat the olive oil in a 4-quart soup pot or Dutch oven over medium heat. Add the celery and shallots and season with a pinch of salt and freshly ground black pepper. Cook, stirring frequently, until the vegetables begin
to soften but not brown, 4 to 6 minutes.

2. Add the garlic and marjoram and cook until fragrant, 1 minute more.

3. Add the carrots, potatoes, and tomatoes, stirring to incorporate with the seasonings and aromatics, then add 2 cups of broth, partially cover, and simmer until the vegetables are just barely tender, 10 to 20 minutes.

4. Add the beans, the reserved tomato juices, and the remaining 1 cup of broth. Stir to combine and simmer, partially covered, for 10 minutes to meld the flavors.

5. Taste the soup and adjust the seasoning with the vinegar, salt, and pepper.

6. Ladle the soup into bowls, garnish each serving with chives, and serve.

*Tip:* If you have time, consider cooking dried beans for the soup. Freshly cooked beans tend to retain their shape better and are plumper, creamier, and truer to their natural flavor than canned. You can save cooking time by presoaking dried beans for 4 hours, which allows them to soften. Always discard the soaking water and start with fresh water for cooking. One-half cup dry beans (most kinds) yields 1½ cups cooked beans, the amount in a 15-ounce can.

**Per Serving:** Calories: 472; Fats: 10g; Protein: 28g; Cholesterol: 0mg; Carbohydrates: 69g; Fiber: 16g; Sodium: 323mg

# Chicken and Rice Stew

DAIRY-FREE / PREP TIME: 20 MINUTES / COOK TIME: 50 MINUTES

Here's yet another reason to rely on whole foods, such as brown rice, for your heart healthy way of eating: the oil and fiber in brown rice lowers cholesterol. The difference between white and brown rice is lot more than just color. Whole rice has several layers and only the outer hull is removed to produce brown rice, which leaves most of the fiber and vitamin E rich bran and germ intact. Together with the lean, high quality protein of chicken breast, one serving of this nutrient dense stew can count toward your recommended daily servings of whole grains.

2½ cups low-sodium chicken broth

¼ cup chopped onion

2 garlic cloves, minced

¼ cup sliced celery

½ cup sliced carrots

1 tablespoon chopped fresh parsley

⅛ teaspoon freshly ground black pepper

1 teaspoon dried thyme

1 bay leaf

3 ounces chicken breast, cut into cubes

⅓ cup dry long grain brown rice

2 cups stemmed and deveined kale

2 teaspoons lime juice

1. Combine the chicken broth, onion, garlic, celery, carrots, parsley, pepper, thyme, and the bay leaf in a large saucepan or Dutch oven. Bring to a boil. Reduce the heat to low and simmer until the onion and celery begin to soften, 10 to 15 minutes.

2. Stir the chicken and rice into the simmering broth and cook until the rice is tender and the chicken is cooked through and no longer pink in the middle, about 30 to 35 minutes.

3. Remove the bay leaf and stir in the kale and lime juice. Continue cooking until the kale is tender, 3 to 5 minutes.

4. Serve hot.

*Tip:* Rice is available prepackaged as well as in bulk containers at most grocery stores, making it easy for you to buy only the amount you need. If purchasing brown rice in packaged containers, check to see if there is a "use-by" date on the package since brown rice, owing to its natural oils, has the potential to become rancid if kept too long.

**Per Serving:** Calories: 443; Fats: 11g; Protein: 15g; Cholesterol: 113mg; Carbohydrates: 38g; Fiber: 4g; Sodium: 263mg.

# Moroccan Spiced Red Lentil and Millet Stew

**DAIRY-FREE, GLUTEN-FREE, VEGAN / PREP TIME: 15 MINUTES / COOK TIME: 50 MINUTES**

This uncomplicated and inexpensive stew makes it effortless for you to reach your recommended daily number of servings of colorful vegetables. Spicy and thick, this stew is high in plant-based, fiber-rich protein and B vitamins from lentils and the whole grain millet. Added heart healthy benefits are provided by vitamin A and potassium-rich dried apricots, which add a depth of flavor and texture contrast to this nutritious stew. Balanced in food groups and nutrition, you will only need basic pantry staples to prepare this filling and satisfying meal.

½ tablespoon olive oil

½ cup finely chopped onion

3 cups low-sodium
    vegetable broth

⅓ cup dry millet

1 cup dried lentils, rinsed

1 celery stalk, chopped

½ cup finely chopped
    red bell pepper

2 tablespoons tomato paste

⅛ teaspoon cayenne pepper

1 teaspoon ground coriander

½ teaspoon ground cumin

¼ teaspoon ground cinnamon

½ cup chopped dried apricots

Salt

1. Heat the olive oil in a 3-quart stockpot or saucepan over medium heat. Add the onion and cook stirring frequently, until the onion is fragrant, about 6 minutes.

2. Add the broth, millet, and lentils. Bring the mixture to a boil.

3. Add the celery, bell pepper, tomato paste, cayenne, coriander, cumin, cinnamon, dried apricots, and salt to taste. Turn down the heat, cover and let simmer for 35 to 45 minutes, or until the lentils and millet are tender.

4. Serve hot.

*Tip:* When cooking for two, finding ingredients sold in smaller portions is always a welcome discovery. In the case of tomato paste, which is used as a thickener in this recipe, look for it packed in a squeezable tube. Because the tube is airtight, the paste can be refrigerated for months without spoiling. If you don't have it, substitute 1 tablespoon tomato paste with 2 to 3 tablespoons tomato puree and reduce the liquid in the recipe by 2 to 3 tablespoons.

**Per Serving:** Calories: 573; Fats: 7g; Protein: 33g; Cholesterol: 0mg; Carbohydrates: 96g; Fiber: 35g; Sodium: 429mg.

# Beans and Greens Stew

DAIRY-FREE, GLUTEN-FREE, VEGAN / PREP TIME: 10 MINUTES / COOK TIME: 50 MINUTES

Nothing says comfort food better than a hot and nutritious bowl of beans and greens. It's so easy to put together a hearty, high-protein one-dish meal rich in vitamins, minerals, phytochemicals, and fiber with these two foods to focus on. With their deep red color, kidney beans are exceptionally rich in a type of flavonoid called proanthyocyanidins, a powerful antioxidant that removes free radicals from the body. High in cholesterol lowering fiber, this stew is rich in folate and magnesium, which can help reduce your risk of heart attack. Enjoy this delicious dish with crusty whole-grain bread.

1 tablespoon olive oil

1 large onion, thinly sliced

Salt

2 garlic cloves, minced

1 (15-ounce) can red
    kidney beans

2 cups water

1 (6-ounce) bag baby spinach

1 bay leaf

½ cup tightly packed, coarsely chopped flat-leaf parsley

½ cup tightly packed, coarsely chopped cilantro

1 bunch scallions, thinly sliced
    (about ½ cup)

Freshly ground black pepper

1 lemon cut into wedges and
    juice of 1 lemon for serving

1. Heat the olive oil over medium heat in a heavy soup pot or Dutch oven and add the sliced onion. Cook, stirring often, until it begins to turn color, about 5-6 minutes. Turn the heat to low, add a pinch of salt and continue to cook, stirring often, until the onion is dark brown and has melted down to about half its original volume, about 20 minutes.

2. Add the garlic and cook, stirring, until it is fragrant, about 30 seconds. Add the beans and water and bring to a simmer. Simmer partly covered for 5 minutes.

3. Add the spinach by the handful, stirring until wilted before adding another handful, until all of the spinach has been added. Stir in the bay leaf, parsley, cilantro, and scallions. Simmer for 10 to 15 minutes, until the parsley and cilantro are tender but still bright. Remove the bay leaf. Season with salt and pepper.

4. Serve with lemon wedges and squeeze fresh lemon juice into each bowl.

*Tip:* You can make this stew through step 2 up to 3 days ahead and keep it in the refrigerator, or freeze it up to a month. For the most vibrant flavor, it's best to serve this stew shortly after adding the spinach and herbs. Add the lemon juice right before serving.

**Per Serving:** Calories: 287; Fats: 9g; Protein: 14g; Cholesterol: 0mg; Carbohydrates: 40g; Fiber: 14g; Sodium: 231mg.

# Roasted Squash Bisque with Pistachios

DAIRY-FREE, GLUTEN-FREE, VEGAN / PREP TIME: 5 MINUTES / COOK TIME: 1 HOUR 10 MINUTES

Winter squashes are packed with health-protective carotenoids including beta-carotene, lutein, and zeaxanthin, and as the weather cools and they become available, consider putting winter squash on your weekly autumn menu. High in cholesterol-lowering fiber, winter squash is also an excellent source of the antioxidant vitamins A and C. Butternut, acorn, and Hubbard squash would all work well in this recipe as they all have a sweet almost nutty flavor. Choose soy milk for added protein and for its own unique nutty taste to complement the squash.

1 small winter squash, about 1 pound (about 1½ cups chopped)

1 cup low-sodium vegetable broth

⅛ teaspoon freshly ground black pepper

1 garlic clove, minced

¼ teaspoon ground nutmeg

⅓ cup unsweetened plain plant-based milk

¼ cup finely chopped pistachios

1. Preheat the oven to 375°F.

2. Cut the squash in half and scoop out the seeds. Place the halves on a baking sheet with cut-sides down and prick the skin with a sharp knife. Bake for approximately 1 hour, or until the flesh is tender.

3. Let the squash cool slightly. Scoop out the flesh into a blender or food processor.

4. Add the broth, pepper, garlic, and nutmeg and process until smooth.

5. Pour the soup into a large saucepan and heat over low heat, stirring constantly until it comes to a boil, 3 to 5 minutes. Stir in the milk and continue to cook only until the soup bubbles and is heated through, about 5 minutes.

6. Transfer into soup bowls, garnish with the chopped pistachios, and serve.

*Tip:* If you are in a hurry, you can save time by using cubed fresh squash sold in the produce section of most supermarkets. Boil 1½ cups of cubed squash in water until tender, about 15 minutes, and drain. Transfer the cooked squash into a blender and continue at step 4.

**Per Serving:** Calories: 244; Fats: 13g; Protein: 6g; Cholesterol: 0mg; Carbohydrates: 32g; Fiber: 6g; Sodium: 90mg.

Mushroom Frittata, p. 117

# 6

# Vegetarian Entrées

# Loaded Sweet Potatoes

DAIRY-FREE, GLUTEN-FREE, VEGAN / PREP TIME: 5 MINUTES / COOK TIME: 80 MINUTES

This loaded sweet potato is perfect for an easy weeknight meal. Sweet potatoes are an excellent and inexpensive staple to have on hand. These deep orange-fleshed nutritional powerhouses contain high levels of protein along with a number of heart healthy ingredients including vitamin $B_6$, which breaks down homocysteine, an amino acid that contributes to hardening of the arteries. Stuffed with fiber- and protein-rich black beans, and topped with creamy avocado for healthy fats, this recipe is filling and satisfying.

2 medium sweet potatoes

½ tablespoon olive oil

1 garlic clove, minced

4 cups stemmed and chopped kale leaves

½ cup halved grape tomatoes

⅓ cup water

1 (15-ounce) can black beans, drained and rinsed

Salt

Freshly ground black pepper

½ avocado, peeled, seeded, and sliced

1. Preheat the oven to 375°F and line a baking sheet with parchment paper.

2. Using a fork, poke multiple holes into both sweet potatoes. Place the sweet potatoes on the baking sheet and bake for 45 to 60 minutes, or until tender.

3. In the meantime, heat the olive oil in a medium saucepan over medium heat. Add the garlic and cook for 1 minute, or until fragrant, taking care not to brown it. Add the kale and tomatoes and toss to coat. Add the water, cover, and cook for 5 minutes. Stir the vegetables, decrease the heat, and cook, uncovered, 15 minutes more until the kale is bright green and slightly wilted.

4. Add the beans and cook until warmed through. Season with salt and pepper.

5. Cut the sweet potatoes in half lengthwise. Top with the black bean–kale mixture and sliced avocado. Serve hot.

*Perfectly Portioned Plate:* Serve the sweet potatoes with a side of roasted Brussels sprouts (can be roasted with the potatoes) and a fresh green salad.

**Per Serving:** Calories: 751; Fats: 15g; Protein: 28g; Cholesterol: 0mg; Carbohydrates: 133g; Fiber: 33g; Sodium: 163mg

# Tofu Kale Scramble

DAIRY-FREE, GLUTEN-FREE, VEGAN, QUICK & EASY / PREP TIME: 15 MINUTES / COOK TIME: 15 MINUTES

This tofu scramble is high in complete protein from the soy, and rich in cholesterol-lowering fiber and cardioprotective B vitamins, calcium, potassium, magnesium, folate, and niacin from the kale. Nutritional yeast adds a cheesy flavor while antioxidant-rich turmeric adds a vibrant yellow color. For the best results, press the block of tofu between paper towels with a plate on top to remove excess water before cooking. Filling and nutritious, enjoy this with a grain-based side dish.

½ teaspoon olive oil

⅓ cup diced red bell pepper

½ cup packed, stemmed, and chopped kale

¼ cup diced scallions, plus more for garnish

1 (14-ounce) block extra-firm tofu, pressed for 10 to 15 minutes

½ cup diced fresh tomato

1 tablespoon plus 1 teaspoon nutritional yeast

¼ teaspoon onion powder

¼ teaspoon garlic powder

⅛ teaspoon salt

⅛ teaspoon freshly ground black pepper

¼ cup diced avocado

¼ teaspoon turmeric, for color (optional)

1. Heat the olive oil in a large sauté pan over medium heat.

2. Add the bell pepper, kale, and scallions to the pan and sauté for about 3 minutes, or until the kale turns bright green and is slightly wilted.

3. Crumble the block of tofu into approximately ½-inch chunks and fold them into the vegetables.

4. Stir in the tomato, nutritional yeast, onion powder, garlic powder, salt, and pepper and simmer over medium-low heat for 2 to 3 minutes.

5. Add the diced avocado and turmeric (if using) and stir for 1 to 2 minutes, just long enough to heat the avocado through.

6. Serve the scramble garnished with some diced scallions.

*Perfectly Portioned Plate:* Serve the scramble with warmed corn tortillas and a side of steamed broccoli.

**Per Serving:** Calories: 206; Fats: 9g; Protein: 21g; Cholesterol: 0mg; Carbohydrates: 14g; Fiber: 5g; Sodium: 287mg

# Creamy Quinoa, Lentils, and Roasted Root Vegetables

DAIRY-FREE, GLUTEN-FREE, VEGAN / PREP TIME: 15 MINUTES / COOK TIME: 45 MINUTES

This hearty and delicious dish has a protein-rich base of creamy quinoa mixed with black lentils and fresh chard topped with simply seasoned roasted rainbow carrots, beets, and crunchy almonds. Fresh parsley adds a pop of color and flavor. With vitamins A and K from the chard; magnesium, folate, fiber, and B vitamins from the lentils; and calcium and vitamin D from the milk, this dish is like a complete multivitamin and mineral supplement for your heart.

*For the lentils*
¼ cup dried black lentils
¾ cup water
Pinch salt

*For the roasted carrots
  and beets*
½ pound rainbow carrots with
  stems (stems optional)
Olive oil nonstick
  cooking spray

2 medium beets, peeled
  and sliced
Salt
Freshly ground black pepper

*For the creamy quinoa*
¾ cup low-sodium
  vegetable broth
¾ cup unsweetened almond
  milk, divided
½ cup quinoa, rinsed
½ teaspoon onion powder
¼ teaspoon garlic powder

1 cup chopped and stemmed
  Swiss chard
1 tablespoon chopped
  fresh parsley, plus
  more for garnish
Salt
Freshly ground black pepper
¼ cup chopped almonds

### TO MAKE THE LENTILS

In a small saucepan over medium heat, add the lentils, water, and salt and bring to a boil. Cover, lower the heat to medium-low, and simmer for 35 to 40 minutes.

### TO MAKE THE ROASTED CARROTS AND BEETS

1.  Preheat the oven to 400°F and line a baking sheet with parchment paper. Wash the carrots well and remove extra roots and leaves, leaving roughly 2 inches of stem. Lightly spray the lined baking sheet with cooking spray, add the carrots and beets, then spray them lightly with cooking spray. Sprinkle with salt and pepper to season.

2.  Roast for 25 to 30 minutes, or until the vegetables are fork-tender and beginning to brown.

### TO MAKE THE CREAMY QUINOA

1.  Heat the vegetable broth, ¼ cup of almond milk, the quinoa, onion powder, and garlic powder in a partially covered wide pan over medium heat. Bring to a boil, reduce the heat to low, and simmer for 15 to 20 minutes, or until the quinoa is soft.

2.  Add the remaining almond milk ¼ cup at a time, cooking and stirring all the while. When all the milk is added and the quinoa has a light creaminess to it, add the cooked lentils, chard, and parsley. Turn off the heat and stir until the chard is slightly wilted. Season with salt and pepper.

3.  Divide between two bowls, top with the roasted vegetables and almonds, garnish with parsley, and serve.

**Per Serving:** Calories: 445; Fats: 11g; Protein: 20g; Cholesterol: 0mg; Carbohydrates: 70g; Fiber: 17g; Sodium: 530mg

# Portobello Mushrooms with Mozzarella and Onions

GLUTEN-FREE / PREP TIME: 10 MINUTES / COOK TIME: 50 MINUTES

Tasty, meaty Portobello mushroom caps are stuffed with shredded part-skim mozzarella cheese and caramelized onions for a delicious vegetarian dish. Low in calories yet high in the essential electrolyte potassium, Portobello mushrooms boast high amounts of heart healthy B vitamins including folate and niacin. And while options for cheese may seem limited on a Mediterranean-style eating plan, part-skim mozzarella is one of the best choices you can make due to its low saturated fat content. Made with just a few simple ingredients, this recipe would make a great Meatless Monday meal.

½ tablespoon olive oil

1½ cups diced onion

Salt

Freshly ground black pepper

2 Portobello mushrooms, stems removed

6 tablespoons shredded part-skim mozzarella cheese

1 cup sliced zucchini

1. Preheat the oven to 350°F and line a baking pan with parchment paper.

2. Heat the olive oil in a medium saucepan over medium heat. Add the onion and cook for about 20 minutes, or until soft and browned. If the onions begin to stick, add a little water and cook until the water evaporates. Season with salt and pepper.

3. Place the mushrooms in the baking pan, stemmed-side up. Pack half of the cooked onions and half of the mozzarella in each mushroom cap.

4. Arrange the sliced zucchini beside the mushrooms in the baking pan. Season with salt and pepper. Bake for 30 minutes and serve warm.

*Perfectly Portioned Plate:* Serve this dish with a salad of fresh baby greens, sliced carrots, and tomatoes.

**Per Serving:** Calories: 171; Fats: 8g; Protein: 10g; Cholesterol: 11mg; Carbohydrates: 19g; Fiber: 5g; Sodium: 139mg

# Indian Spiced Cauliflower Fried "Rice"

**DAIRY-FREE, GLUTEN-FREE, QUICK & EASY / PREP TIME: 10 MINUTES / COOK TIME: 10 MINUTES**

Cauliflower "rice" has become a mainstream staple for people wanting to boost their intake of vegetables. Available in the produce section of supermarkets, riced cauliflower is simply cauliflower that is chopped small enough to mimic grains of rice. A fantastic starch substitute, nutritious cauliflower is a great way to keep calories in check while adding more veggies to your diet. This recipe is an Indian-inspired version of fried rice that is high in protein, fiber, and anti-inflammatory antioxidants. Full of flavor, it is a bowl of delicious, aromatic comfort food.

2 teaspoons olive oil, divided

2 eggs, beaten

2 garlic cloves, finely minced

¼ cup finely chopped
    red bell pepper

¼ cup finely chopped carrots

¼ cup finely chopped onion

3 cups grated cauliflower

1 cup frozen shelled edamame

½ teaspoon ground cumin

¼ teaspoon ground ginger

⅛ teaspoon ground cardamom

⅛ teaspoon ground cinnamon

Freshly ground black pepper

1 cup finely chopped
    fresh spinach

2 teaspoons Bragg's liquid
    aminos (or low-sodium
    soy sauce)

¼ cup cashews, for garnish

1. Heat 1 teaspoon of olive oil in a large sauté pan. Add the eggs and slowly stir until curds form, then fold the curds over themselves until there is no more liquid egg. Remove from the heat and break into small pieces. Transfer the eggs to a plate.

2. Heat the remaining 1 teaspoon of olive oil. Add the garlic and sauté for 30 seconds. Add the bell pepper, carrots, and onion and sauté for 2 minutes. Add the cauliflower, edamame, cumin, ginger, cardamom, cinnamon, and a few grinds of pepper and cook, stirring, for 5 to 8 minutes. Add the spinach and cook until wilted, about 2 minutes.

3. Add the Bragg's aminos and the cooked egg and stir well to combine. Remove from the heat and divide equally between two bowls. Sprinkle with the cashews and serve.

*Perfectly Portioned Plate:* Serve this dish with a plate of sliced cucumbers and tomatoes drizzled with balsamic vinegar.

**Per Serving:** Calories: 386; Fats: 22g; Protein: 27g; Cholesterol: 186mg; Carbohydrates: 29g; Fiber: 11g; Sodium: 473mg

# Tofu Vegetable Stir-Fry

**DAIRY-FREE / PREP TIME: 15 MINUTES / COOK TIME: 45 MINUTES**

Tofu is an excellent source of high-quality complete plant-based protein, and when cooked properly, yields the perfect texture and flavor. The trick to working with tofu is to drain and press it to remove excess water and then bake it at a high temperature to brown it and create a tougher texture. This makes it more "meat-like" and allows it to better soak up the delicious sauce seasoning it. You'll be surprised at how good this simple and nutritious stir-fry tastes.

*For the sauce*

2 teaspoons low-sodium
    soy sauce

3 to 4 tablespoons water

1 tablespoon peeled and
    grated fresh ginger

1 tablespoon honey

1 tablespoon rice wine vinegar

1 tablespoon cornstarch

*For the stir-fry*

1 (14-ounce) package firm or
    extra-firm tofu, drained
    for 15 minutes

1 tablespoon olive oil

1 cup diced red bell pepper

1 cup broccoli florets

1 cup snow peas

TO MAKE THE SAUCE

In a small mixing bowl, whisk together all the sauce ingredients and set it aside.

TO MAKE THE STIR-FRY

1.  Preheat the oven to 400°F and line a baking sheet with parchment paper, or lightly grease the baking sheet.

2.  Chop the tofu into 1-inch cubes and spread them on the prepared baking sheet. Bake for 25 to 35 minutes, flipping halfway through to ensure even cooking.

3.  Once the tofu is golden brown and a bit firm, remove it from the oven and set it aside to dry while you prepare the vegetables.

4.  Heat the olive oil in a large skillet over medium-high heat. Add the bell pepper, broccoli, and snow peas and cook, stirring often, for 5 to 7 minutes. Give the sauce a quick stir and when the vegetables have some color and are softened, add the sauce to the pan and stir. It should bubble and thicken.

5.  Add the tofu and stir to coat. Cook the mixture for 3 to 5 minutes, stirring often. When the veggies are cooked to your liking, remove from the heat and serve.

*Perfectly Portioned Plate:* This dish is perfect served over brown rice for a more filling meal. Start cooking the rice when you start baking the tofu.

**Per Serving:** Calories: 331; Fats: 16g; Protein: 21g; Cholesterol: 0mg; Carbohydrates: 31g; Fiber: 7g; Sodium: 344mg

# Spicy Spinach and Almond Stir-Fry

**DAIRY-FREE, QUICK & EASY / PREP TIME: 10 MINUTES / COOK TIME: 10 MINUTES**

This Thai-inspired stir-fry uses lime, cilantro, and sriracha to add bold flavors and a spicy kick to sautéed spinach and vegetables. Crunchy sliced almonds add inflammation-reducing heart healthy fats, while protein-rich eggs bring the ingredients together. For best results, cook your rice in advance and refrigerate it until you are ready to start cooking, as stir-fries work best with chilled rice. You'll need about two-thirds of a cup of dried rice to yield two cups cooked.

3 teaspoons olive oil, divided

2 eggs, beaten

2 garlic cloves, minced

¾ cup chopped scallions

1 cup thinly sliced
  Brussels sprouts

4 cups baby spinach

¼ cup sliced almonds

2 cups cooked and chilled
  brown rice

2 teaspoons reduced-sodium
  tamari or soy sauce

2 teaspoons sriracha

1 lime, halved

¼ cup chopped fresh cilantro,
  for garnish

1. Heat a large (12-inch or wider) wok or nonstick frying pan over medium-high heat. Once the pan is hot enough that a drop of water sizzles on contact, add 1 teaspoon of olive oil. Pour in the eggs and cook, stirring occasionally, until the eggs are scrambled and lightly set, about 3 minutes. Transfer the eggs to a medium bowl.

2. Add 1 teaspoon of olive oil to the pan and add the garlic, scallions, and Brussels sprouts. Cook, stirring frequently, for 30 seconds, or until fragrant. Add the spinach and continue to cook, stirring frequently, for about 2 minutes, or until the spinach is wilted and tender. Transfer the mixture to the bowl of eggs.

3. Add the almonds to the pan and cook, stirring frequently, for about 1 minute, or until they are crisp and lightly browned. Add the remaining 1 teaspoon of olive oil and the rice to the pan and cook, stirring occasionally, for about 3 minutes until the rice is hot.

4. Pour the contents of the bowl back into the pan. Add the tamari, sriracha, and juice from half a lime. Stir to combine and remove from the heat.

5. Cut the remaining lime half into wedges then divide the stir-fry into individual bowls. Garnish with the lime wedges and a sprinkling of cilantro. Serve immediately.

*Perfectly Portioned Plate:* Serve this dish with a side salad of crispy romaine, grated carrots, and fresh tomato slices.

**Per Serving:** Calories: 587; Fats: 20g; Protein: 20g; Cholesterol: 164mg; Carbohydrates: 86g; Fiber: 9g; Sodium: 557mg

# Pocket Eggs with Sesame Sauce

DAIRY-FREE, QUICK & EASY / PREP TIME: 5 MINUTES / COOK TIME: 5 MINUTES

Pocket eggs are a traditional dish in China including the Taiwan province of China and are simply eggs that are cooked and folded and served with a quick sauce. The sauce in this recipe uses black sesame seeds, which add a nutritional punch as well as a nutty, delicate flavor to this high-protein dish. Sesame seeds have the highest amount of cholesterol-lowering phytosterols of nearly all nuts and seeds. Phytosterol benefits are so dramatic that they are sometimes added to processed foods as butter replacements. Skip the processed stuff and enjoy the natural benefits of whole foods in this flavorful, fast dish.

2 teaspoons low-sodium
   soy sauce

1 teaspoon sesame oil

1½ tablespoons rice vinegar

1 tablespoon minced scallions

2 teaspoons olive oil

4 large eggs

1 tablespoon black or white
   sesame seeds

1 tablespoon dried basil

¼ teaspoon freshly ground
   black pepper

1. In a small bowl, whisk together the soy sauce, sesame oil, vinegar, and scallions. Set it aside.

2. Heat the olive oil in a medium nonstick skillet over medium heat and swirl to coat. Crack 2 eggs into a small bowl then crack the remaining 2 eggs into a second small bowl.

3. Working quickly, pour 2 eggs on one side of the skillet and the other 2 on the opposite side of the skillet. The egg whites will flow together, forming one large piece.

4. Sprinkle the sesame seeds, basil, and pepper over the eggs. Cook until the egg whites are crispy and golden brown on the bottom and the yolks are firmly set, about 3 minutes. Keeping them in one piece, flip the eggs using a wide spatula and cook until the whites turn crispy and golden brown on the other side, 1 to 2 minutes more.

5. Pour the reserved sauce over the eggs. Simmer for 30 seconds, turning the eggs once to coat both sides with sauce. Serve in wedges, drizzled with the pan sauce.

*Perfectly Portioned Plate:* This dish is traditionally served over rice. Choose brown rice for the most fiber, vitamins, and minerals.

**Per Serving:** Calories: 241; Fats: 19g; Protein: 14g; Cholesterol: 372mg; Carbohydrates: 3g; Fiber: 1g; Sodium: 440mg

# Lentil Walnut Burgers

DAIRY-FREE, GLUTEN-FEE, QUICK & EASY / PREP TIME: 10 MINUTES, PLUS 10 MINUTES CHILLING TIME
COOK TIME: 10 MINUTES

This delicious burger is made from powerhouse lentils combined with fiber- and B vitamin–rich brown rice and omega-3–packed walnuts. Quick to prepare, the patties use basic pantry ingredients combined in a food processor. You can even customize the recipe, adding your favorite veggies to the mix. If you like, bake the burgers in a 400°F oven for 15 minutes, flip, and bake for another 10 minutes until golden.

½ cup chopped red onion

⅓ cup walnuts

¼ cup packed fresh
    cilantro leaves

1 garlic clove, minced

¼-inch piece fresh ginger,
    peeled

¾ teaspoon ground coriander

¾ teaspoon ground cumin

½ teaspoon paprika

⅛ teaspoon salt

¾ cup cooked brown rice

1 (15-ounce) can lentils,
    drained and rinsed, divided

1 egg, beaten

1 teaspoon olive oil,
    plus a drizzle

3 tablespoons gluten-free
    oat flour

1 cup chopped romaine leaves

1. In a food processor, add the onion, walnuts, cilantro, garlic, and ginger and process until finely chopped.

2. Add the coriander, cumin, paprika, salt, rice, and half the lentils and pulse a few times until well combined. Transfer to a bowl and add the remaining lentils. Add the egg and olive oil and mix until combined. Add the oat flour and mix to combine. Chill in the refrigerator for 10 minutes.

3. Shape the mixture into 4 well-packed patties. Heat a large skillet over medium-high heat and add a drizzle of olive oil. Place the patties in the skillet and cook for 4 to 6 minutes on each side.

4. Divide the romaine leaves equally between two serving plates. Top each pile of romaine with 2 burgers and serve warm.

*Perfectly Portioned Plate:* Serve these burgers with a side of steamed mixed vegetables such as green beans, carrots, mushrooms, and broccoli seasoned with a dash of Bragg's aminos and olive oil.

**Per Serving:** Calories: 561; Fats: 19g; Protein: 31g; Cholesterol: 82mg; Carbohydrates: 72g; Fiber: 21g; Sodium: 189mg

# Savory Cheesy Rosemary Oatmeal

GLUTEN-FREE, QUICK & EASY / PREP TIME: 5 MINUTES / COOK TIME: 15 MINUTES

Oatmeal is one of the best foods you can eat to lower cholesterol. It is high in soluble fiber: the type that helps bind cholesterol for excretion. Oats also have other cardioprotective benefits due to their unique mix of antioxidants, which can lower inflammation in the body. And while oats are associated with breakfast, oatmeal is mild in flavor and holds up to toppings, making it suitable for savory flavors. In this recipe, lots of veggies are added to the oats along with creamy ricotta cheese, a heart healthy low-fat choice.

1 cup gluten-free rolled oats

1 cup water

1 cup unsweetened almond milk or nonfat milk

⅔ cup frozen green peas

1 teaspoon olive oil

½ cup sliced button mushrooms

1 cup firmly packed chopped baby spinach

1 cup chopped tomato

1 tablespoon fresh rosemary

½ cup part-skim ricotta cheese

Salt

Freshly ground black pepper

1. In a medium pot over medium heat, bring the oats, water, and almond milk to a boil, stirring occasionally. Add the peas, decrease the heat to medium low, and cook for 1 to 2 minutes, stirring often to prevent sticking and burning. Decrease the heat to low.

2. Meanwhile, heat the olive oil in a medium skillet over medium heat. Add the mushrooms and spinach and sauté for 3 to 4 minutes, or until the mushrooms start to release their liquid and the spinach is slightly wilted.

3. Add the tomato and rosemary to the mushroom-spinach mixture and cook for 3 minutes.

4. Add the ricotta to the oats and stir to combine. Transfer the vegetable mixture to the oat mixture and stir until well incorporated. Season with salt and pepper and serve warm.

*Perfectly Portioned Plate:* Serve this dish with a salad made with crispy romaine lettuce, sliced carrots, and crunchy radishes.

**Per Serving:** Calories: 393; Fats: 11g; Protein: 21g; Cholesterol: 22mg; Carbohydrates: 50g; Fiber: 9g; Sodium: 243mg

# Edamame Burritos

DAIRY-FREE, QUICK & EASY / PREP TIME: 15 MINUTES / COOK TIME: 15 MINUTES

This creative spin on traditional burritos uses high-protein and fiber-rich edamame (green soybeans) combined with eggs and vitamin C–packed peppers for a filling, healthy, and satisfying vegetarian meal. Edamame is naturally gluten-free and low calorie, contains no cholesterol, and is an excellent source of protein, iron, and calcium. Rich in phytochemicals called isoflavones, soy protein has been shown to lower cholesterol, reducing the risk for heart disease. You can customize this recipe with your favorite burrito toppings.

Olive oil nonstick
    cooking spray
1 cup shelled edamame
½ cup sliced red, yellow,
    or green bell pepper
½ cup diced onion
2 garlic cloves, minced
2 eggs
2 egg whites
Salt
Freshly ground black pepper
½ cup chopped fresh tomato
1 teaspoon ground cumin
2 (7-inch) whole-wheat tortillas
½ cup shredded romaine lettuce
½ cup sliced avocado

1. Spray a large skillet with cooking spray and heat over medium-high heat. Add the edamame, bell pepper, onion, and garlic to the skillet and sauté for 7 to 8 minutes, or until the onion is translucent and the edamame is cooked through.

2. While the edamame mixture is cooking, whisk the eggs and egg whites in a bowl. Season with salt and pepper.

3. Add the tomato and cumin to the skillet and cook for 1 to 2 minutes, stirring frequently.

4. Add the eggs to the skillet and cook for 2 to 3 minutes, or until the mixture appears solid at the bottom. Break up the mixture with a spatula and cook for 2 to 3 more minutes, or until cooked to your liking.

5. Place a tortilla on each serving plate and top with half of the mixture. Top with the romaine lettuce and avocado and roll into a burrito. Serve warm.

*Perfectly Portioned Plate:* Serve these burritos with quinoa for added protein and fiber, and to make a balanced, complete meal.

**Per Serving:** Calories: 434; Fats: 21g; Protein: 29g; Cholesterol: 164mg; Carbohydrates: 37g; Fiber: 11g; Sodium: 212mg

# Zucchini "Spaghetti" with Almond Pesto

DAIRY-FREE, GLUTEN-FREE, VEGAN, QUICK & EASY / PREP TIME: 10 MINUTES / COOK TIME: 10 MINUTES

Fresh, bright zucchini substitutes for pasta in this simple and nutritious dish. Heart healthy dairy-free almond pesto is tossed with warm zucchini noodles to create a light yet filling meal. Zucchini, also called *courgette* in some parts of the world, is low in calories yet high in essential nutrients like potassium, the antioxidant vitamins A and C, and a type of fiber called pectin that can lower cholesterol levels. With added protein from green peas, this quick and easy recipe can help you meet your recommended daily servings of vegetables.

1 cup loosely packed fresh basil leaves, divided

⅓ cup roasted, unsalted almonds

½ tablespoon sherry vinegar

⅛ teaspoon salt

1 teaspoon olive oil

2 garlic cloves, minced

½ red onion, sliced

1 cup green peas (fresh or frozen and thawed)

2 medium zucchini, julienned or cut into long noodles with spiralizer or vegetable peeler

1. Add ½ cup of basil, the almonds, vinegar, and salt to a food processor. Pulse, scraping down the sides of the food processor frequently, until a smooth paste forms. Scrape into a bowl and set it aside.

2. Heat the olive oil in a medium skillet over medium heat. Add the garlic, onion, and peas and sauté for 2 to 4 minutes, or until the onion is translucent and the peas are cooked through.

3. Add the zucchini noodles to the skillet and cook for 1 to 2 minutes, stirring frequently. Add the pesto to the skillet, toss to combine, and cook for 1 to 2 minutes, or just enough to warm through.

4. Remove from the heat and divide between two plates, top with the remaining ½ cup of basil leaves, and serve.

*Perfectly Portioned Plate:* Serve this dish with a salad of mixed baby greens, sliced tomatoes, and sliced carrots.

**Per Serving:** Calories: 220; Fats: 11g; Protein: 11g; Cholesterol: 0mg; Carbohydrates: 24g; Fiber: 9g; Sodium: 173mg

# One-Skillet Southwest Quinoa and Vegetables

DAIRY-FREE, GLUTEN-FREE, VEGAN / PREP TIME: 10 MINUTES / COOK TIME: 30 MINUTES

This easy recipe has the flavors of the Southwest mixed with sautéed vegetables and quinoa to create a heart healthy meal that cooks in one skillet. Loaded with cholesterol-lowering fiber from the corn, beans, and quinoa, and high in energy-sustaining plant protein, this nutritious mix of vegetables contains high amounts of the inflammation-reducing antioxidant vitamins A and C. Corn is especially rich in a type of phytonutrient shown to reduce blood pressure, which can reduce risk for heart disease. With only one dish to clean up, this dish is perfect for a speedy weeknight dinner.

½ tablespoon olive oil

½ cup chopped sweet onion

¼ cup chopped red bell pepper

1 cup chopped tomato, with juices

½ cup quinoa, rinsed

½ cup water

½ cup corn kernels, fresh or thawed from frozen

1 (15-ounce) can black beans, drained and rinsed

½ teaspoon chili powder

½ teaspoon ground cumin

Salt

Freshly ground black pepper

¼ cup chopped fresh cilantro, for garnish (optional)

Avocado slices, for garnish (optional)

1 lime, sliced, for garnish (optional)

1. In a large skillet, heat the olive oil over medium heat. Sauté the onion and bell pepper for 3 to 4 minutes, or until softened.

2. Add the tomato with its juices, quinoa, water, corn, black beans, chili powder, and cumin and season with salt and pepper. Bring the quinoa mixture to a boil. Decrease the heat and simmer, covered, for 20 to 25 minutes, or until the liquid has been absorbed.

3. Remove from the heat and divide between two serving plates. Garnish with the cilantro, avocado slices, and fresh lime (if using) and serve warm.

*Perfectly Portioned Plate:* Serve this dish with a fresh salad of baby spinach, sliced mushrooms, and sliced carrots.

**Per Serving:** Calories: 533; Fats: 8g; Protein: 28g; Cholesterol: 0mg; Carbohydrates: 93g; Fiber: 24g; Sodium: 102mg

# Farro with Sundried Tomatoes, Pine Nuts, and Arugula

DAIRY-FREE, VEGAN / PREP TIME: 5 MINUTES / COOK TIME: 40 MINUTES

While quinoa gets most of the attention as one of the most nutritious whole grains, farro is quickly gaining in popularity. A little softer in texture, farro is high in protein and fiber, and is a good source of heart healthy nutrients including niacin and magnesium. Farro does contain gluten, however, as it is a type of unprocessed wheat. Cooked to perfection in one skillet with phytonutrient-rich arugula, tomatoes, and pine nuts, this nutritious dish is a snap to prep and clean up.

½ tablespoon olive oil

1 large shallot, diced

¼ cup julienned water-packed sundried tomatoes, drained

4 ounces uncooked farro

1 cup low-sodium vegetable broth

2 to 3 cups loosely packed arugula

4 or 5 large fresh basil leaves, thinly sliced

¼ cup pine nuts

1. Heat the olive oil in a large skillet over medium-high heat. Add the shallot and sauté for about 5 minutes, until golden.

2. Add the sundried tomatoes and farro to the skillet and sauté for about 30 seconds to toast the farro.

3. Add the vegetable broth, stir to combine, and bring the mixture to a boil. Decrease the heat to low, cover, and simmer for 30 minutes, or until the farro is tender.

4. Stir in the arugula and basil and cook for 1 to 2 minutes, or until wilted. Add the pine nuts and toss to combine. Serve warm.

*Perfectly Portioned Plate:* Serve this dish with a side of steamed green beans.

**Per Serving:** Calories: 350; Fats: 17g; Protein: 13g; Cholesterol: 41mg; Carbohydrates: 39g; Fiber: 2g; Sodium: 239mg

# Braised Lentils and Vegetables

DAIRY-FREE, GLUTEN-FREE, VEGAN / PREP TIME: 15 MINUTES / COOK TIME: 60 MINUTES

Braising usually involves searing meat or chicken, adding a little liquid, lowering the heat, and letting it cook for a long time. We use the same technique in this recipe with fennel, carrots, and French green lentils. When you slow cook foods, it really allows the flavors to develop, and lentils are perfect cooked this way. The lentils add protein and fiber, while fennel adds folate, potassium, fiber, and antioxidant vitamins A and C for a dish that packs a heart healthy punch.

½ tablespoon olive oil

¾ cup diced onion

2 garlic cloves, minced

1 celery stalk, thinly sliced

4 ounces baby carrots

½ cup sliced mushrooms

1 fennel bulb, cut into
    8 wedges

¾ cup dried green French
    lentils du Puy (or brown
    lentils), rinsed well
    and drained

¼ cup water

1½ cups unsalted
    vegetable stock

2 fresh thyme sprigs

1 fresh rosemary sprig

Salt

Freshly ground black pepper

Fresh parsley leaves,
    for garnish

1. Heat a deep 4-quart saucepan over medium-high heat. Add the olive oil and heat for 20 to 30 seconds. Add the onion, decrease the heat to medium, and cook, stirring often, for about 5 minutes, or until the onion starts to soften and turn golden. Add the garlic and celery and continue cooking for about 5 more minutes, stirring occasionally.

2. Add the carrots, mushrooms, fennel, lentils, and water and cook for 2 to 3 minutes, stirring until the water is completely absorbed.

3. Add the stock, thyme, and rosemary. Cover the pan with a tight-fitting lid and decrease the heat to low. The liquid should barely simmer. Cook for 40 to 45 minutes, or until the lentils are not too mushy or too firm and the liquid is mostly absorbed. Season with salt and pepper and serve garnished with fresh parsley.

*Perfectly Portioned Plate:* To complete this meal, serve it with a side of steamed green cruciferous vegetables such as broccoli and Brussels sprouts, and crusty whole-grain bread.

**Per Serving:** Calories: 399; Fats: 6g; Protein: 26g; Cholesterol: 0mg; Carbohydrates: 64g; Fiber: 28g; Sodium: 345mg

# Tarragon Sweet Potato and Egg Skillet

DAIRY-FREE, GLUTEN-FREE, QUICK & EASY / PREP TIME: 5 MINUTES / COOK TIME: 20 MINUTES

The licorice taste of tarragon combined with earthy sweet potatoes and acidic tomatoes creates a one-skillet dish as delicious as it is simple to prepare. Eggs provide lots of protein, and they sit atop sweet potatoes that are full of heart healthy nutrients including antioxidant beta-carotene and mineral potassium. To keep added fats and sodium in check, nutritional yeast replaces cheese. You can also customize the seasonings to your preferences.

½ tablespoon olive oil

2 medium sweet potatoes, cut into ½-inch chunks (about 5 inches long)

1 teaspoon dried tarragon

⅛ teaspoon salt

⅛ teaspoon freshly ground black pepper

⅓ cup water

½ cup diced tomato

¼ cup nutritional yeast or low-fat cheese

2 large eggs

¼ cup thinly sliced scallions

1. Heat the olive oil in a medium skillet over medium heat. Add the sweet potatoes and sprinkle with the tarragon, salt, and pepper. Stir, cover, and cook for about 5 minutes, stirring halfway through. Stir in the water and tomato, cover again, and cook for about 10 more minutes, or until the potatoes are tender, stirring occasionally. If the skillet starts to get too dry, add a bit more water, 1 to 2 tablespoons at a time.

2. When the potatoes are tender, sprinkle the nutritional yeast evenly over the top.

3. Make two small wells in the sweet potatoes, leaving a few sweet potatoes at the bottom of each well. Break 1 egg into each well. Cover the skillet, decrease the heat to medium-low or low, and cook for about 6 minutes, or until the eggs are set and the yolks are cooked to your liking.

4. Remove from the heat and sprinkle with the scallions. Serve warm.

*Perfectly Portioned Plate:* Serve this dish with sautéed summer squash and a salad of mixed baby greens.

**Per Serving:** Calories: 437; Fats: 11g; Protein: 14g; Cholesterol: 20mg; Carbohydrates: 66g; Fiber: 10g; Sodium: 330mg

# Black-Eyed Pea Collard Wraps with Ginger Peanut Sauce

DAIRY-FREE, GLUTEN-FREE, QUICK & EASY / PREP TIME: 10 MINUTES

This creative recipe uses sturdy collard green leaves as a wrap for the nourishing legume, black-eyed peas. Look for fresh black-eyed peas in the produce section, or you can buy the more convenient frozen or canned; whatever the form, they are loaded with health benefits. High in cholesterol-lowering fiber, potassium for healthy blood pressure, and protein to keep you feeling full, the peas in this recipe are topped with a delicious peanut and ginger sauce to give the wraps an Asian flair. Super easy and super nutritious, this recipe takes just minutes to prepare.

*For the sauce*

⅓ cup unsalted natural peanut butter

2 tablespoons rice vinegar

1 teaspoon honey

1 tablespoon peeled and grated ginger

2 tablespoons water

Dash sriracha

Salt

*For the wraps*

6 large collard leaves, washed and dried

⅓ cup grated carrots

1 cucumber, peeled and julienned

1 (15-ounce) can black-eyed peas, drained and rinsed

TO MAKE THE SAUCE

In a small bowl, whisk together all the ingredients for the sauce, making sure to smooth out any lumps from the peanut butter.

TO MAKE THE WRAPS

1. Trim the center stem of each collard leaf lengthwise so it is more flexible. Spread a spoonful of the peanut sauce on the inner side of each leaf, then layer a sixth of the carrots, cucumber, and black-eyed peas on each leaf.

2. To wrap, fold in the sides of the leaf and roll it up as you would a burrito. Secure each wrap with a toothpick. Place three wraps on each plate and serve.

*Perfectly Portioned Plate:* To complete this meal, serve it with a side of whole-wheat soba noodles seasoned with any remaining peanut ginger sauce.

**Per Serving:** Calories: 343; Fats: 22g; Protein: 14g; Cholesterol: 0mg; Carbohydrates: 26g; Fiber: 7g; Sodium: 131mg

# Braised Cauliflower, Butter Beans, and Squash Penne

DAIRY-FREE, VEGAN, QUICK & EASY / PREP TIME: 10 MINUTES / COOK TIME: 20 MINUTES

Contrary to popular belief, pasta is a truly nutritious food; you just have to choose whole-grain varieties and stick to 2-ounce portion sizes. Whole-wheat pasta is rich in fiber, heart healthy B vitamins, and slowly digested carbohydrates for energy. In this recipe, whole-wheat penne is cooked in broth and almond milk and simmered with creamy butternut squash, antioxidant-rich cauliflower, and fiber- and protein-filled butter beans, commonly called lima beans. Made in just one pot, the result is a silky, toothsome, satisfying meal.

1½ teaspoons olive oil

2 garlic cloves, minced

1 teaspoon dried thyme

⅛ teaspoon red pepper flakes

1 cup low-sodium
     vegetable broth

1 cup unsweetened
     almond milk

4 ounces whole-wheat penne

1 cup (1-inch pieces)
     cauliflower florets

1 cup (1-inch cubes) peeled
     butternut squash

1 cup fresh butter beans, or
     canned, drained and rinsed

Freshly ground black pepper

1. Heat the olive oil in a medium saucepan over medium-high heat. Add the garlic, thyme, and red pepper flakes and cook, stirring, for 1 minute. Add the broth, almond milk, penne, cauliflower, squash, and beans. Bring to a boil, decrease the heat, and cook at a lively simmer, uncovered, for 10 to 15 minutes, or until the pasta is tender and the liquid has thickened and is greatly reduced.

2. Remove from the heat, stir in some pepper, and let it stand for 5 minutes. Serve warm.

*Perfectly Portioned Plate:* Serve this dish with a salad of crispy romaine lettuce, diced tomatoes, sliced carrots, mushrooms, and a drizzle of olive oil.

Per Serving: Calories: 447; Fats: 6g; Protein: 19g; Cholesterol: 0mg; Carbohydrates: 79g; Fiber: 12g; Sodium: 475mg

# Mushroom Frittata

GLUTEN-FREE, QUICK & EASY / PREP TIME: 10 MINUTES / COOK TIME: 20 MINUTES

Also known as an "Italian omelet," this simple dish makes an excellent "need in a hurry" dinner, breakfast, lunch, or brunch. Shiitake mushrooms add a rich, smoky flavor and a number of health-promoting properties including immune and cardiovascular support. High in B vitamins, shiitake mushrooms are a concentrated source of the antioxidant minerals selenium and zinc, and a good source of vitamin D and cholesterol-lowering fiber. Seasoned with the bright flavors of fresh herbs, this heart healthy dish is as versatile as it is tasty.

4 eggs, slightly beaten

1 tablespoon chopped fresh basil

⅛ teaspoon salt

¼ teaspoon freshly ground black pepper

1 tablespoon olive oil

2 cups chopped shiitake mushrooms

⅓ cup chopped scallions

¼ cup shredded low-fat Cheddar cheese

Sprigs of fresh thyme, for garnish

Basil leaves, for garnish

1. In a medium bowl, combine the eggs, basil, salt, and pepper. Set it aside.

2. Heat the olive oil in a small, nonstick skillet. Add the mushrooms and scallions. Cook, uncovered and stirring occasionally, for about 5 minutes, or until the mushrooms are soft.

3. Preheat the broiler.

4. Pour the egg mixture over the vegetables in the skillet. Cook over medium heat and as the egg mixture sets, run a spatula around the sides so that uncooked egg can slide underneath. Continue until the egg mixture is almost set, about 10 minutes; the surface should be just a little moist. Sprinkle the cheese over the top.

5. Place the skillet 4 to 5 inches from the heat source and broil for 1 to 2 minutes, or until the top is set and the cheese has melted.

6. Serve topped with sprigs of thyme and basil.

*Perfectly Portioned Plate:* Serve the frittata with a salad of fresh baby spinach, arugula, tomatoes, and carrots.

**Per Serving:** Calories: 330; Fats: 19g; Protein: 19g; Cholesterol: 379mg; Carbohydrates: 23g; Fiber: 4g; Sodium: 348mg

# Acorn Squash Stuffed with White Beans and Kale

DAIRY-FREE, GLUTEN-FREE / PREP TIME: 10 MINUTES / COOK TIME: 25 MINUTES

An acorn squash's natural shape makes it perfect for stuffing with nutritious fillings, and one squash is the perfect serving size for two people. Acorn squash is an excellent source of the antioxidant vitamin C, and is high in vitamin A, and heart healthy B vitamins including niacin, folate, and B$_6$. Filled with protein- and fiber-rich beans that are seasoned with Mediterranean herbs and a touch of feta cheese, this is a satisfying and hearty vegetarian meal.

1 medium acorn squash, halved and seeded

2½ teaspoons olive oil, divided

⅛ teaspoon salt

¼ teaspoon freshly ground black pepper, divided

¼ cup chopped onion

2 garlic cloves, minced

1 tablespoon water

1 tablespoon tomato paste, no salt added

4 cups stemmed and chopped kale

1 cup canned white beans, drained and rinsed

2 tablespoons wheat germ

1 tablespoon dried basil

1 teaspoon dried rosemary

2 tablespoons feta cheese

1. Cut a small slice off the bottom of each squash half so they rest flat. Brush the insides with ½ teaspoon of olive oil, then sprinkle with the salt and ⅛ teaspoon black pepper. Place in an 8-by-8-inch (or similar size) microwave-safe dish. Cover with plastic wrap and microwave on high until the squash is fork-tender, about 12 minutes.

2. Meanwhile, heat 1 teaspoon of olive oil in a large skillet over medium heat. Add the onion and cook, stirring, for 2 to 3 minutes, or until the onion starts to brown. Add the garlic and cook, stirring, for 1 minute. Stir in the water, tomato paste, and the remaining ⅛ teaspoon of pepper. Stir in the kale, cover, and cook for 3 to 5 minutes, or until tender. Stir in the beans and cook until heated through, 1 to 2 minutes more. Remove from the heat.

3.  Position a rack in the center of the oven and preheat the broiler.

4.  In a bowl, combine the wheat germ, basil, rosemary, feta cheese, and the remaining 1 teaspoon of olive oil. Fill each squash half with half of the kale-bean mixture. Place them in a baking pan or on a baking sheet. Sprinkle them with the wheat germ mixture and broil for 1 to 2 minutes, or until the wheat germ has browned. Serve warm.

*Perfectly Portioned Plate:* Serve with a mixed green salad with radicchio and red onion.

**Per Serving:** Calories: 401; Fats: 10g; Protein: 18g; Cholesterol: 8mg; Carbohydrates: 68g; Fiber: 16g; Sodium: 328mg

Tarragon Salmon Fillets and Tomato Cucumber Medley, p. 140

# 7

# Chicken & Fish Entrées

# Baked Mustard-Lime Chicken

**DAIRY-FREE, GLUTEN-FREE / PREP TIME: 10 MINUTES, PLUS AT LEAST 15 MINUTES CHILLING TIME
COOK TIME: 20 MINUTES**

When you are looking for a great source of lean, low-fat, high-quality protein, chicken breast is an excellent choice, especially when you're trying to cut down on red meat consumption. All of the B vitamins are present in chicken, along with over half your recommended daily amount of the antioxidant mineral selenium. Healthy and nutritious, this recipe for chicken breast is full of flavorful lime and cilantro, and baking it allows the flavors to entirely infuse into the dish.

¼ cup freshly squeezed
　　lime juice
¼ cup chopped fresh cilantro
2 garlic cloves, minced
2 tablespoons Dijon mustard
½ tablespoon olive oil
½ tablespoon chili powder
⅛ teaspoon salt
¼ teaspoon freshly ground
　　black pepper
2 (4-ounce) skinless, boneless
　　chicken breasts

1.　Preheat the oven to 350°F.

2.　Add the lime juice, cilantro, garlic, mustard, olive oil, chili powder, salt, and pepper to a food processor and pulse until the ingredients are well combined.

3.　Place the chicken breasts in a 7-by-11-inch glass oven-proof baking dish. Pour the marinade over the chicken, cover, and refrigerate for at least 15 minutes or up to 6 hours.

4.　Bake, uncovered, for 18 to 20 minutes, or until an instant-read thermometer registers 165°F. Serve immediately.

*Perfectly Portioned Plate:* Serve this dish with a side of roasted Brussels sprouts, which can cook while the chicken is baking.

**Per Serving:** Calories: 189; Fats: 5g; Protein: 27g; Cholesterol: 65mg; Carbohydrates: 4g; Fiber: 2g; Sodium: 423mg

# Chicken with Mushroom Sauce

DAIRY-FREE, QUICK & EASY / PREP TIME: 5 MINUTES / COOK TIME: 15 MINUTES

Mushrooms contain high levels of vitamin D and fiber, which helps lower cholesterol. Here, they are used to make a savory sauce to enliven basic sautéed chicken breasts into true comfort food at its finest. The shallots add vitamins, minerals, fiber, and heart healthy polyphenolic compounds. Full of satiating protein, this meal can be prepared in a snap.

1 tablespoon olive oil, divided

2 (6-ounce) skinless, boneless chicken breasts

¼ teaspoon salt, divided

⅛ teaspoon freshly ground black pepper

¼ cup chopped shallots

4 ounces button mushrooms, sliced

1 portobello mushroom, sliced

2 garlic cloves, minced

¼ cup dry white wine, cooking wine, or low-sodium broth

1 teaspoon flour

½ cup water

2 teaspoons minced fresh thyme

1. Heat 1 teaspoon of olive oil in a large nonstick skillet over medium-high heat, swirling to coat. Sprinkle the chicken with ⅛ teaspoon salt and the pepper. Add the chicken to the skillet and cook for about 3 minutes on each side, or until an instant-read thermometer registers 165°F. Transfer the chicken to a serving platter and keep warm.

2. Add the shallots and mushrooms to the skillet and sauté, stirring occasionally, for about 4 minutes, or until browned. Add the garlic and sauté for 1 minute, stirring constantly. Add the wine and stir, scraping the pan to loosen any browned bits from the bottom. Bring to a boil and cook until the liquid almost evaporates.

3. Sprinkle the mushroom mixture with the remaining ⅛ teaspoon of salt and the flour and cook for about 30 seconds, stirring constantly. Add the water to the skillet and bring to a boil. Cook for 2 minutes more, or until slightly thick. Remove the skillet from the heat, add the remaining 2 teaspoons of olive oil and the thyme, and stir until combined.

4. Serve the sauce over the chicken.

*Perfectly Portioned Plate:* Serve the chicken breasts atop cooked quinoa and spoon the pan sauce on top. Prepare a salad of fresh baby greens, sliced carrots, tomatoes, and red onions to complete the meal.

**Per Serving:** Calories: 329; Fats: 10g; Protein: 44g; Cholesterol: 97mg; Carbohydrates: 12g; Fiber: 2g; Sodium: 414mg

# Asian Chicken Lettuce Wraps

DAIRY-FREE / PREP TIME: 5 MINUTES, PLUS 1 HOUR MARINATING TIME / COOK TIME: 20 MINUTES

This nutritious recipe combines intense Asian taste with a few simple, healthy ingredients for a filling high-protein wrap. An intensely flavored marinade is used to season lean chicken breast, and butter lettuce leaves, which add fiber, B vitamins, and the antioxidant vitamins A and C, are used in place of the typical bready wrap. Garnished with heart healthy nuts, these wraps will keep you energized and satisfied.

½ tablespoon olive oil

½ tablespoon dark sesame oil

½ tablespoon rice vinegar

½ tablespoon low-sodium
  soy sauce

1 teaspoon chili sauce
  (such as sriracha)

1 teaspoon peeled and grated
  fresh ginger

½ teaspoon freshly grated
  lime zest

1 garlic clove, minced

2 (6-ounce) skinless, boneless
  chicken breasts

Olive oil nonstick cooking spray

4 Boston lettuce leaves

½ cup fresh mint leaves

½ cup bean sprouts

½ cup sliced red bell pepper

2 tablespoons chopped
  peanuts

1 lime, cut into 4 wedges

1. In a small bowl, whisk together the olive oil and sesame oil, vinegar, soy sauce, chili sauce, ginger, lime zest, and garlic. Reserve 1 tablespoon of the mixture. Add the remaining mixture to a large resealable bag. Add the chicken breasts, seal the bag, and marinate in the refrigerator for 1 hour, turning occasionally. Remove the chicken from the bag and discard the marinade.

2. Heat a large nonstick grill pan over medium-high heat. Coat the pan with cooking spray. Add the chicken and grill for about 12 minutes, or until an instant-read thermometer registers 165°F, turning once halfway through. Let it stand for 5 minutes before thinly slicing.

3. Divide the chicken among the lettuce leaves. Top each lettuce leaf with mint, sprouts, bell pepper, and ½ teaspoon of the reserved dressing. Garnish with the chopped peanuts, wrap like a burrito, and serve with the lime wedges.

*Perfectly Portioned Plate:* Serve these wraps with cooked short-grain brown rice and steamed green beans.

**Per Serving:** Calories: 346; Fats: 14g; Protein: 45g; Cholesterol: 97mg; Carbohydrates: 11g; Fiber: 3g; Sodium: 415mg

# Cilantro-Lime Chicken and Avocado Salsa

DAIRY-FREE, GLUTEN-FREE / PREP TIME: 10 MINUTES, PLUS 30 MINUTES MARINATING TIME
COOK TIME: 12 MINUTES

Preparing homemade salsa with fresh ingredients is a great way to add nutrients to your diet and dress up meats and poultry without using processed ingredients. This recipe delivers big on flavor by marinating chicken breasts in a zesty sauce of cilantro and lime, and topping them with fresh salsa made with heart healthy avocados. High in lean protein, this recipe is certain to become a family favorite.

*For the chicken*

2 tablespoons minced fresh cilantro

1½ tablespoons freshly squeezed lime juice

2 teaspoons olive oil

⅛ teaspoon salt

½ teaspoon ground cumin

2 (6-ounce) skinless, boneless chicken breasts

Olive oil nonstick cooking spray

*For the salsa*

½ cup chopped plum tomato

¼ cup chopped red bell pepper

1 tablespoon finely chopped onion

2 tablespoons minced fresh cilantro

2 tablespoons freshly squeezed lime juice

1 small peach, peeled and finely chopped

⅛ teaspoon salt

⅛ teaspoon freshly ground black pepper

½ avocado, peeled and finely chopped

**TO MAKE THE CHICKEN**

1. In a medium bowl, combine the cilantro, lime juice, olive oil, salt, and cumin. Add the chicken to the marinade and toss to coat. Refrigerate for 30 minutes. Remove the chicken from the marinade and discard the marinade.

2. Heat a large nonstick skillet or grill pan over medium-high heat. Coat the skillet with cooking spray. Add the chicken to the pan and cook for 6 minutes on each side, or until an instant-read thermometer registers 165°F.

**TO MAKE THE SALSA**

In a medium bowl, combine the tomato, bell pepper, onion, cilantro, lime juice, peach, salt, and pepper. Add the avocado and stir gently to combine. Serve the chicken topped with the salsa.

*Perfectly Portioned Plate:* Serve this dish with a side of brown rice and a fresh salad of mixed baby greens. Start cooking the rice when you begin marinating the chicken.

**Per Serving:** Calories: 366; Fats: 17g; Protein: 41g; Cholesterol: 97mg; Carbohydrates: 15g; Fiber: 6g; Sodium: 411mg

# Moroccan Spiced Chicken with Sweet Onions

DAIRY-FREE, GLUTEN-FREE / PREP TIME: 5 MINUTES, PLUS 10 MINUTES MARINATING TIME
COOK TIME: 20 MINUTES

This exotically flavored recipe uses a mix of spices to make *ras el hanout,* which is a blend common in North African cooking and is especially popular in Moroccan cuisine. While the composition of the mixture varies, the core ingredients are ones found in most cooks' spice racks. Sweet onions are the ideal ingredients to contrast the strong spices used to season the chicken breasts. Rich in natural antioxidants and phytochemicals from the spices, this nutritious high-protein dish will transport you on a weeknight culinary adventure.

1 teaspoon ground cinnamon

1 teaspoon paprika

¾ teaspoon ground cumin

½ teaspoon ground cardamom

½ teaspoon ground coriander

½ teaspoon ground ginger

½ teaspoon ground turmeric

1 tablespoon olive oil, divided

2 (6-ounce) skinless, boneless
   chicken breasts

⅛ teaspoon salt

Olive oil nonstick
   cooking spray

1 cup sliced yellow onion

1 teaspoon honey

1. In small bowl, mix together the cinnamon, paprika, cumin, cardamom, coriander, ginger, and turmeric.

2. Heat ½ tablespoon of olive oil in a large ovenproof skillet over medium-low heat, swirling to coat. Add the spice mixture to the skillet and cook, stirring frequently, for about 3 minutes, or until toasted. In a large resealable bag, combine the spice mixture and chicken breasts, seal, and shake well to coat the chicken. Marinate the chicken in the refrigerator for 10 minutes.

3. Preheat the oven to 350°F.

4.  Remove the chicken from the bag and sprinkle with the salt. Heat the skillet over medium-high heat and lightly coat it with cooking spray. Add the chicken and cook for about 4 minutes. Turn the chicken over and cook for 1 minute more. Remove the chicken from the pan.

5.  Add the remaining ½ tablespoon of olive oil to the pan, swirling to coat. Add the onion and sauté for 2 minutes, or until it starts to brown. Return the chicken to the pan and drizzle the honey over all.

6.  Bake for 10 minutes, or until an instant-read thermometer registers 165°F. Serve immediately.

*Perfectly Portioned Plate:* Serve this dish with roasted vegetables and brown rice. Try stirring in a spoonful of tahini for a punch of flavor.

**Per Serving:** Calories: 295; Fats: 10g; Protein: 40g; Cholesterol: 97mg; Carbohydrates: 11g; Fiber: 3g; Sodium: 261mg

# Grilled Chicken Breasts with Plum Salsa

DAIRY-FREE, GLUTEN-FREE, QUICK & EASY / PREP TIME: 5 MINUTES / COOK TIME: 12 MINUTES

Including a wide variety of fruits, vegetables, and lean proteins in your diet is the best way to ensure you provide your body with an array of health-protective nutrients. By "eating a rainbow" of foods at each meal, you can also lower your risk for chronic disease. Spice-rubbed grilled chicken flavors come together with the sweet plum salsa and a touch of spice from the hot sauce. Substitute peaches, nectarines, or pineapples in place of the plums, if you prefer.

*For the chicken*

1 teaspoon brown sugar

¼ teaspoon ground cumin

¼ teaspoon garlic powder

⅛ teaspoon salt

1 teaspoon olive oil

2 (6-ounce) skinless, boneless chicken breasts

*For the plum salsa*

1 cup chopped ripe plum

2 tablespoons chopped fresh cilantro

2 tablespoons chopped red onion

2 tablespoons chopped red bell pepper

2 teaspoons cider vinegar

¼ teaspoon hot sauce

⅛ teaspoon salt

TO MAKE THE CHICKEN

1. In a small bowl, combine the brown sugar, cumin, garlic powder, and salt. Rub the chicken all over with the mixture.

2. Heat the olive oil in a nonstick skillet or grill pan over medium heat. Add the chicken and cook for 6 minutes per side, or until an instant-read thermometer registers 165°F.

TO MAKE THE PLUM SALSA

In a medium-size bowl, combine all the salsa ingredients. Serve the salsa over the chicken.

*Perfectly Portioned Plate:* Serve this dish with a fresh salad of mixed baby greens and roasted red potatoes.

**Per Serving:** Calories: 265; Fats: 5g; Protein: 41g; Cholesterol: 97mg; Carbohydrates: 16g; Fiber: 2g; Sodium: 424mg

# Balsamic Rosemary Chicken

**DAIRY-FREE, GLUTEN-FREE / PREP TIME: 10 MINUTES, PLUS 45 MINUTES CHILLING TIME**
**COOK TIME: 35 MINUTES**

Balsamic vinegar with garlic and rosemary is used to make a low-sodium, simple reduction sauce that goes wonderfully with chicken. Balsamic vinegar has a dark, rich color and a sweet, pungent taste due to the lengthy aging process. Rich in polyphenols and antioxidants, balsamic vinegar neutralizes free radicals, promotes healthy cholesterol levels, and may be beneficial for blood pressure.

½ cup balsamic vinegar,
    plus 2 tablespoons
1 teaspoon olive oil
1 tablespoon chopped
    fresh rosemary
1 garlic clove, minced
⅛ teaspoon salt
Freshly ground black pepper
Olive oil cooking spray
2 (6-ounce) boneless, skinless
    chicken breasts
Fresh rosemary sprigs,
    for garnish

1. In a small saucepan, stir together ½ cup of balsamic vinegar, the olive oil, rosemary, garlic, salt, and pepper. Bring to a boil, lower the heat to medium, and simmer for about 3 minutes, or until reduced by half. Transfer the pan to the refrigerator for about 15 minutes or the freezer for about 5 minutes.

2. Coat a 9-by-9-inch baking dish with cooking spray. Place the chicken in the baking dish and pour the cooled marinade over the chicken. Refrigerate for 30 minutes.

3. Preheat the oven to 400°F. Remove the dish from the refrigerator, cover it with aluminum foil and bake the chicken in the marinade for 35 minutes, or until an instant-read thermometer registers 165°F.

4. Transfer the chicken to serving plates. Pour the cooked marinade into a small saucepan. Add the remaining 2 tablespoons of balsamic vinegar and cook for 3 to 5 minutes, or until the sauce has thickened. Pour the sauce over the chicken and serve garnished with fresh rosemary.

*Perfectly Portioned Plate:* Serve this dish with steamed broccoli, quinoa, and a fresh salad of mixed baby greens.

**Per Serving:** Calories: 228; Fats: 4g; Protein: 39g; Cholesterol: 97mg; Carbohydrates: 2g; Fiber: 1g; Sodium: 261mg

# Salmon and Summer Squash in Parchment

**DAIRY-FREE, GLUTEN-FREE / PREP TIME: 15 MINUTES / COOK TIME: 17 MINUTES**

Salmon is one of the best choices you can make when deciding which fish to choose to reach your recommended two servings per week. Salmon is unusually high in omega-3 fatty acids, with a 4-ounce portion containing about 2 grams, which meets the daily amount recommended by the American Heart Association. This recipe uses parchment to wrap salmon and summer squash, allowing the fish and vegetables to steam in their own juices, locking in aroma and flavor. Individually portioned with no dishes to wash, this recipe makes including salmon in your diet a breeze.

2 tablespoons freshly squeezed lemon juice

1 cup sliced yellow summer squash

2 tablespoons sliced shallot

1 tablespoon chopped fresh oregano leaves

½ tablespoon olive oil

⅛ teaspoon salt

⅛ teaspoon freshly ground black pepper

1 cup sliced medium zucchini

2 (6-ounce) skinless salmon fillets

1 teaspoon grated lemon zest, divided

1. Preheat the oven to 400°F.

2. In a medium bowl, combine the lemon juice, yellow squash, shallot, oregano, olive oil, salt, and pepper.

3. Place 2 large parchment rectangles on the work surface with the short side of the parchment closest to you. On half of one parchment rectangle, arrange half the zucchini slices lengthwise, overlapping them slightly. Place a salmon fillet on the zucchini, sprinkle with half the lemon zest, then top with half the yellow squash mixture. Fold the parchment over the ingredients. Repeat with the other piece of parchment and the remaining ingredients. To seal the packets, begin at one corner and tightly fold over the edges about ½ inch all around, overlapping the folds.

4. Place the packets on a baking sheet and bake for about 17 minutes, or until the salmon turns opaque throughout.

5. To serve, carefully cut the packets open, being careful to avoid escaping steam, and with a spatula gently transfer the salmon and vegetables to two plates. Spoon any liquid remaining in the parchment over the salmon and vegetables.

*Perfectly Portioned Plate:* Serve this dish with a side of quick-cooking whole-wheat couscous and a salad of mixed baby greens and tomatoes.

**Per Serving:** Calories: 291; Fats: 15g; Protein: 35g; Cholesterol: 75mg; Carbohydrates: 7g; Fiber: 2g; Sodium: 238mg

# Rainbow Trout Baked in Foil
# with Tomatoes and Thyme

DAIRY-FREE, GLUTEN-FREE, QUICK & EASY / PREP TIME: 10 MINUTES / COOK TIME: 15 MINUTES

Less expensive than salmon yet equally nutritious, rainbow trout gets the silver medal for one full gram of omega-3 fatty acids. Trout also boasts more than twice the RDA for vitamin $B_{12}$, and half the RDA for niacin, a B vitamin crucial to maintaining healthy cholesterol levels and keeping homocysteine levels in check. Wrapped in foil with vitamin C–rich tomatoes and aromatic thyme, this dish can be prepped in advance and kept in the refrigerator until shortly before cooking.

1½ teaspoons olive oil, divided, plus more for greasing the foil
2 small rainbow trout, deboned
Salt
Freshly ground black pepper
1 cup peeled, seeded, and chopped tomato
2 garlic cloves, minced
4 fresh thyme sprigs
Freshly chopped parsley, for garnish
Freshly chopped thyme, for garnish
Lemon wedges, for serving

1. Preheat the oven to 450°F. Cut two sheets of heavy-duty aluminum foil into squares that are 3 inches longer than your fish. Grease the dull side of the foil with olive oil and place a trout, skin-side down, on each square. Season both sides with salt and pepper and open them flat.

2. In a bowl, combine the tomato, garlic, and 1 teaspoon of olive oil and season with salt and pepper. Spoon equal amounts over the middle of each trout. Place 2 thyme sprigs on top of each, and fold the two sides of the trout together. Drizzle ¼ teaspoon of olive oil over each fish.

3.  Making sure the trout are in the middle of each square, fold the foil up loosely, grab it at the edges, and crimp together tightly to make a packet. Place them on a baking sheet and bake for 10 to 15 minutes, checking one of the packets after 10 minutes. The flesh should be opaque and pull apart easily when tested with a fork.

4.  Place each packet on a plate. Carefully cut across the top to open the packets, taking care not to let the steam burn you. Gently remove the fish from the packets and pour the juices over. Sprinkle with parsley and thyme and serve with lemon wedges.

*Perfectly Portioned Plate:* Serve this dish with an arugula salad and steamed asparagus drizzled with freshly squeezed lemon juice.

**Per Serving:** Calories: 320; Fats: 16g; Protein: 39g; Cholesterol: 105mg; Carbohydrates: 5g; Fiber: 1g; Sodium: 177mg

# Sesame-Crusted Tuna Steaks

DAIRY-FREE, GLUTEN-FREE, QUICK & EASY / PREP TIME: 5 MINUTES / COOK TIME: 12 MINUTES

Tuna steaks are another heart healthy fish choice, ranking close to salmon in their omega-3 fatty acid content. Not only is tuna an excellent source of lean protein and packed to the gills with B vitamins, it also tastes great and can be made into dozens of dishes. This recipe combines the omega-3 power of tuna with the cholesterol-lowering power of phytosterol-rich sesame seeds. Just 5 minutes to prepare and 12 minutes to cook, this dish is perfect for those busy nights when you need a healthy dinner fast.

Olive oil nonstick
   cooking spray
½ tablespoon olive oil
1 teaspoon sesame oil
2 (6-ounce) ahi tuna steaks
6 tablespoons sesame seeds
Salt
Freshly ground black pepper

1. Preheat the oven to 450°F and lightly spray a baking sheet with cooking spray.

2. In a small bowl, stir together the olive oil and sesame oil. Brush the tuna steaks with the oil mixture.

3. Put the sesame seeds in a shallow bowl. Press the steaks into the seeds, turning to cover all sides.

4. Place the tuna steaks on the prepared baking sheet. Sprinkle with salt and pepper. Bake for 4 to 6 minutes per ½-inch thickness of fish, or until the fish begins to flake when tested with a fork. Serve immediately.

*Perfectly Portioned Plate:* Serve the tuna steaks with avocado slices and a side of steamed green beans and button mushrooms.

**Per Serving:** Calories: 520; Fats: 30g; Protein: 56g; Cholesterol: 83mg; Carbohydrates: 6g; Fiber: 3g; Sodium: 166mg

# Salmon and Scallop Skewers

DAIRY-FREE, GLUTEN-FREE / PREP TIME: 30 MINUTES, PLUS 1 HOUR MARINATING TIME
GRILL TIME: 12 MINUTES

This recipe combines two heart healthy favorites—salmon and scallops—in a recipe for grilled skewers that combines the sweet flavors of pineapple with the savory flavors of fish. While scallops are not as high in omega-3 fats as other fish, eating any kind of seafood means you're cutting other protein sources from your diet that may be higher in unhealthy fats, and that's a plus. Scallops are also very mild in flavor, so are a good entry point for those who are not particularly fond of fish. Though grilled in this recipe, these skewers would also taste great cooked under the broiler.

1 (8-ounce) can pineapple chunks in 100% pineapple juice, drained, reserving 2 tablespoons juice

1 tablespoon freshly squeezed lemon juice

1 tablespoon snipped fresh tarragon or 1 teaspoon dried tarragon

¼ teaspoon dry mustard

⅛ teaspoon salt

4 ounces skinless, boneless wild salmon fillets, cut into 1-inch cubes

4 ounces scallops

1 zucchini, cut into ½-inch-thick slices

1 red bell pepper, cut into 1-inch squares

1 red onion, cut into 1-inch pieces

8 button mushrooms

1. Preheat an outdoor grill.

2. In a small bowl, combine the 2 tablespoons of reserved pineapple juice, the lemon juice, tarragon, mustard, and salt. Place the salmon and scallops in a resealable bag, add the marinade and seal the bag. Turn the fish and scallops to coat well. Marinate in the refrigerator for 1 to 2 hours, turning once.

3. Meanwhile, in a small saucepan, bring just enough water to cover the zucchini (1 to 2 inches) to a boil. Add the zucchini and cook, covered, for 3 to 4 minutes, or until nearly tender. Drain and cool.

4. Remove the seafood from the bag, reserving the marinade. On 4 metal skewers, alternately thread the salmon, scallops, zucchini, bell pepper, onion, mushrooms, and pineapple. Brush with the reserved marinade.

5. Grill, uncovered, directly over medium coals for 8 to 12 minutes, turning once, until the scallops turn opaque and the salmon flakes easily when tested with a fork.

6. Serve two skewers on each dinner plate.

*Perfectly Portioned Plate:* Serve these skewers with a side of quinoa and a fresh salad of mixed baby greens.

**Per Serving:** Calories: 260; Fats: 5g; Protein: 26g; Cholesterol: 44mg; Carbohydrates: 32g; Fiber: 6g; Sodium: 285mg

# Flounder Tacos with Cabbage Slaw

**DAIRY-FREE, GLUTEN-FREE, QUICK & EASY / PREP TIME: 10 MINUTES / COOK TIME: 6 MINUTES**

Flounder is readily available and a great choice, with almost half a gram of heart healthy omega-3 fats per serving, 100 percent of your daily RDA of the antioxidant mineral selenium, and lots of vitamin $B_{12}$. Seasoned with a dash of cumin and cooked quickly in a pan, this flounder is served with vitamin C–packed cabbage and heart healthy avocado in corn tortillas for a Mexican-inspired meal.

8 ounces skinless flounder
    fillets, cut into
    1-inch chunks
1 teaspoon ground cumin
⅛ teaspoon salt
⅛ teaspoon freshly ground
    black pepper
1 cup thinly sliced red cabbage
½ avocado, chopped
2 tablespoons freshly squeezed
    lime juice
3 teaspoons olive oil, divided
4 corn tortillas, warmed
Fresh cilantro, for garnish

1. In a small bowl, mix together the flounder, cumin, salt, and pepper.

2. In another small bowl, mix together the cabbage, avocado, lime juice, and 1 teaspoon of olive oil.

3. Heat the remaining 2 teaspoons of olive oil in a medium-size skillet over medium-high heat. Add the flounder to the skillet and cook, turning, for about 4 minutes, or until the fish is just opaque and flakes easily with a fork.

4. Place 2 warm tortillas on each serving plate. Divide the fish among the tortillas and top with the cabbage-avocado slaw. Serve garnished with fresh cilantro.

*Perfectly Portioned Plate:* Serve this dish with a side of black beans seasoned with cilantro, garlic, lime, and cumin.

**Per Serving:** Calories: 413; Fats: 20g; Protein: 32g; Cholesterol: 77mg; Carbohydrates: 28g; Fiber: 7g; Sodium: 299mg

# Lemon Garlic Mackerel

DAIRY-FREE, GLUTEN-FREE, QUICK & EASY / PREP TIME: 10 MINUTES / COOK TIME: 5 MINUTES

Mackerel is another great choice when it comes to selecting oily fish high in omega-3 fats. This slim torpedo-shaped fish contains over 1 gram of omega-3 fatty acids per 3-ounce serving, along with high amounts of B vitamins important for heart health, and the antioxidants selenium and coenzyme Q10. Select the smaller species such as Atlantic or Pacific and not King Mackerel, which tends to be high in mercury. Readily available and full of health benefits, mackerel is seasoned with basic pantry staples and baked to perfection in this quick and easy recipe.

2 (4-ounce) mackerel fillets

Salt

2 garlic cloves, minced

Juice of ½ lemon

Freshly ground black pepper

1. Line a baking sheet with aluminum foil and lay the fillets on it. Sprinkle them with salt and leave them for 5 minutes. This helps give the fish a firmer texture.

2. Meanwhile, preheat the broiler.

3. In a small bowl, mix together the garlic, lemon juice, and some pepper. Pour the mixture over the mackerel.

4. Broil for about 5 minutes, or until the fish is opaque and flakes easily with a fork. Serve immediately.

*Perfectly Portioned Plate:* While the mackerel is cooking, steam slices of fresh zucchini, broccoli, carrots, yellow squash, and mushrooms in a steamer basket. Season simply with lemon juice, black pepper, and a dash of olive oil.

**Per Serving:** Calories: 302; Fats: 20g; Protein: 27g; Cholesterol: 85mg; Carbohydrates: 1g; Fiber: 0g; Sodium: 172mg

# Broiled Tuna Steaks with Peppercorn-Lime Rub

**DAIRY-FREE, GLUTEN-FREE, QUICK & EASY / PREP TIME: 5 MINUTES / COOK TIME: 8 MINUTES**

Tuna gets spiced up in this recipe with a lively four-ingredient rub. Get your fill of cardio-protective omega-3 fatty acids by preparing this speedy dish as part of your heart healthy eating plan. Fresh tuna season runs from late spring to early fall, but frozen steaks are available year round. Select the freshest fish possible and plan to use it the same day or else freeze it.

Olive oil nonstick
    cooking spray
2 (6-ounce) tuna steaks
1 teaspoon freshly grated
    lime zest
⅛ teaspoon salt
½ teaspoon freshly ground
    black pepper
1 garlic clove, minced
Lemon wedges, for serving

1. Preheat the broiler and coat the broiler pan with cooking spray.

2. Place the fish in the prepared broiler pan.

3. In a small bowl, combine the lime zest, salt, pepper, and garlic. Sprinkle the mixture over the fish. Broil for 7 to 8 minutes, or until the fish flakes easily when tested with a fork or is cooked to your liking.

4. Transfer each steak to a serving plate and serve with lemon wedges.

*Perfectly Portioned Plate:* Serve the tuna with a quinoa vegetable salad by combining cooked quinoa with chopped zucchini, red bell pepper, mushrooms, carrots, fresh chopped chives, olive oil, and season with salt and pepper.

**Per Serving:** Calories: 317; Fats: 11g; Protein: 51g; Cholesterol: 83mg; Carbohydrates: 1g; Fiber: 0g; Sodium: 233mg

# Oven-Roasted Salmon Fillets

DAIRY-FREE, GLUTEN-FREE, QUICK & EASY / PREP TIME: 5 MINUTES / COOK TIME: 15 MINUTES

If you want heart healthy yet "easy, fancy" it doesn't get much better than roasted salmon fillets. This is the kind of recipe you want to keep in your back pocket, since once you make it you will never wonder what to do with salmon again. One of the best sources of inflammation-reducing essential omega-3 fatty acids, salmon is full of high-quality protein for long lasting satiety. Salmon is also high in vitamin D, low levels of which are linked to an increased risk of cardiovascular disease.

1 (6-ounce) salmon fillet, cut into 2 pieces
Salt
Freshly ground black pepper
1 lemon, cut into wedges, for garnish
Parsley, for garnish

1. Preheat the oven to 450°F.
2. Season the salmon with salt and pepper. Place the salmon skin-side down on a nonstick baking sheet or in a nonstick pan with an ovenproof handle. Bake until it is cooked through and flakes easily with a fork, 12 to 15 minutes.
3. Serve with the lemon wedges and fresh parsley.

*Perfectly Portioned Plate:* Serve the salmon over almond rice: In a small pan over medium heat, toast $1/4$ cup slivered almonds until lightly browned. Cook brown rice according to directions, cover, and let it stand until the water has been absorbed. Stir in the almonds and season with salt and pepper. Sprinkle with parsley.

**Per Serving:** Calories: 113; Fats: 5g; Protein: 17g; Cholesterol: 38mg; Carbohydrates: 0g; Fiber: 0g; Sodium: 118mg

# Tarragon Salmon Fillets and Tomato Cucumber Medley

QUICK & EASY / PREP TIME: 15 MINUTES / COOK TIME: 15 MINUTES

A little heat makes crispy vitamin B–filled cucumbers slightly creamy, helping to soak up the gently seasoned mixture in this protein- and omega-3–rich recipe. The salmon is warmed up with spices and then cooled down with a refreshing topping of a seasoned yogurt sauce. An added crunch and fiber boost comes from whole-grain breadcrumbs to create a balanced and heart healthy meal.

1 tablespoon olive oil, divided, plus more for oiling

2 (6-ounce) salmon fillets

¼ teaspoon salt, divided

¼ teaspoon freshly ground black pepper, divided

1 tablespoon freshly squeezed lemon juice, plus 1 teaspoon

¼ cup minced shallots

1 tablespoon coarsely chopped fresh tarragon, plus 1 tablespoon fresh tarragon leaves

¼ cup red wine vinegar

4 ounces thin-skinned cucumber, such as English or Persian, sliced

2 medium tomatoes, sliced

2 tablespoons chopped flat-leaf parsley

¼ cup plain nonfat Greek yogurt

1 small garlic clove, grated

1 teaspoon freshly grated lemon zest

¼ cup toasted whole-grain breadcrumbs

1. Preheat the oven to 375°F. Line a baking sheet with aluminum foil and lightly oil it.

2. Sprinkle the salmon with ⅛ teaspoon salt, ⅛ teaspoon of pepper, ½ tablespoon of olive oil, and 1 tablespoon of lemon juice. Place it skin-side down on the baking sheet.

3. Bake the salmon until barely opaque but still moist in the center of the thickest part, 10 to 13 minutes, then remove it from the oven and keep it warm.

4. While the salmon bakes, combine the shallots, chopped tarragon, and vinegar in a small frying pan. Boil over high heat, stirring often until the vinegar evaporates but the shallots still look wet, 4 to 5 minutes. Add ½ tablespoon of olive oil, the remaining ⅛ teaspoon of salt, the remaining ⅛ teaspoon of pepper, the cucumber and tomatoes, and cook for 1 to 2 minutes until softened. Remove from the heat and stir in the parsley.

5.  In a small bowl, combine the yogurt, garlic, lemon zest, and remaining 1 teaspoon of lemon juice. Set it aside.

6.  Divide the tomato-cucumber mixture between two serving plates. Top each plate with a piece of salmon, half of the yogurt dressing, and half of the toasted bread crumbs. Garnish with the fresh tarragon leaves and enjoy.

*Perfectly Portioned Plate:* Serve with a side of roasted Brussels sprouts and quinoa.

**Per Serving:** Calories: 418; Fats: 19g; Protein: 40g; Cholesterol: 77mg; Carbohydrates: 24g; Fiber: 3g; Sodium: 502mg

Pork Chops with Tomato and Fennel Sauce, p. 155

# 8

# Pork & Beef Entrées

# Smothered Pork Chops with Rosemary and Thyme

QUICK & EASY / PREP TIME: 5 MINUTES / COOK TIME: 15 MINUTES

Although often referred to as "the other white meat," pork is technically red meat and so should be consumed in moderation to reduce heart disease risk. That said, lean cuts of pork can be a healthy addition to any diet as pork is high in protein and rich in many vitamins and minerals essential to heart health. Some of those vitamins and minerals include thiamin, niacin, $B_6$, $B_{12}$, and the antioxidant mineral selenium. The gravy in this recipe, made using nonfat milk and low-sodium broth, smothers the pork chops, creating a flavorful, low-fat, high-protein meal.

½ cup low-sodium or unsalted beef broth, divided

2 tablespoons nonfat milk or plant-based milk

2 teaspoons oat flour

2 teaspoons Dijon mustard

⅛ teaspoon salt

⅛ teaspoon freshly ground black pepper

4 (2-ounce) boneless center-cut loin pork chops (about ¼-inch thick)

¼ teaspoon paprika

½ teaspoon dried thyme

½ teaspoon dried rosemary

Olive oil nonstick cooking spray

2 garlic cloves, minced

½ cup sliced button mushrooms

½ cup chopped onion

¼ cup water

¼ cup white cooking wine

1 tablespoon minced fresh parsley, for garnish

1. In a small bowl, whisk together ¼ cup of broth, the milk, flour, mustard, salt, and pepper and set it aside.

2. Sprinkle one side of each pork chop with the paprika, thyme, and rosemary. Heat a large nonstick skillet over medium-high heat. Coat the skillet with cooking spray. Add the pork chops to the skillet and sauté for about 2 minutes on each side, or until an instant-read thermometer registers 145°F. Remove the chops from the skillet.

3. Decrease the heat to medium, add the garlic, mushrooms, and onion and sauté for about 4 minutes, or until lightly golden. Add the remaining ¼ cup of broth, the water, and wine. Bring to a boil and cook for about 2 minutes. Whisk in the reserved milk mixture. Add the pork, turning to coat, and cook for about 1 minute.

4. Transfer to two serving plates, sprinkle with the parsley, and serve warm.

*Perfectly Portioned Plate:* Serve this dish with a salad of mixed baby greens, a side of steamed green beans, and cauliflower mashed "potatoes."

**Per Serving:** Calories: 439; Fats: 29g; Protein: 29g; Cholesterol: 98g; Carbohydrates: 8g; Fiber: 2g; Sodium: 234mg

# Chili-Lime Pork Tenderloin

**DAIRY-FREE / PREP TIME: 5 MINUTES, PLUS 1 HOUR MARINATING TIME / COOK TIME: 30 MINUTES**

When shopping for the leanest cuts of pork, "loin" is the word you want to look for. A 3-ounce cooked portion of pork tenderloin has fewer than 120 calories, fewer than 5 grams of fat, and fewer than 2 grams of saturated fat, making it a good choice to include in a healthy eating plan. Marinated in a spicy, flavorful chili-lime sauce, this tenderloin recipe is full of complete high-quality protein, B vitamins, and essential minerals to keep you feeling satisfied.

1 teaspoon chili powder

2 tablespoons freshly squeezed lime juice

2 tablespoons chopped fresh cilantro

1 teaspoon low-sodium soy sauce

2 garlic cloves, minced

½ teaspoon sugar

8 ounces pork tenderloin

½ tablespoon olive oil

½ avocado, peeled, pitted, and sliced

1. In a small bowl, mix the chili powder, lime juice, cilantro, soy sauce, garlic, and sugar. Using your fingers, rub the mixture thoroughly onto all sides of the tenderloin. Transfer the tenderloin to a dish and refrigerate for 1 hour.

2. Preheat the oven to 400°F.

3. When the pork is marinated, heat the olive oil in a large ovenproof skillet. Add the pork and sear it on all sides, turning with tongs, about 2 minutes total.

4. Transfer the skillet to the oven and bake for 20 to 25 minutes, depending on the thickness of the tenderloin, or until an instant-read thermometer registers 145°F. Baste after about 10 minutes of cooking with any juices that have accumulated, adding 2 tablespoons of water if necessary, to prevent scorching.

5. Transfer the tenderloin to a cutting board, cover loosely with foil, and let it rest for 5 minutes. Slice on the diagonal into ½-inch-thick pieces and serve with the avocado slices.

*Perfectly Portioned Plate:* Serve the tenderloin with a freshly made salsa, brown rice, and steamed broccoli.

**Per Serving:** Calories: 309; Fats: 18g; Protein: 31g; Cholesterol: 83mg; Carbohydrates: 7g; Fiber: 4g; Sodium: 231mg

# Pan-Roasted Pork Tenderloin and Peppers

DAIRY-FREE / PREP TIME: 5 MINUTES / COOK TIME: 25 MINUTES

This colorful and nutritious recipe is prepared in one pan for quick preparation and clean up. Lean, vitamin- and mineral-rich pork tenderloin is cooked with a simple yet delicious sauce and then baked to lock in the flavors. While the pork is baking, peppers rich in vitamin C, fiber, and phytochemicals are lightly sautéed and seasoned with thyme, a nutrient-dense spice containing impressive amounts of vitamins C and A, flavonoid antioxidants, and the minerals iron, manganese, and copper.

*For the pork*

½ tablespoon olive oil

8 ounces pork tenderloin, trimmed

1 teaspoon freshly ground black pepper, divided

¼ teaspoon salt, divided

½ cup unsalted chicken stock

½ teaspoon cornstarch

½ teaspoon cider vinegar

*For the peppers*

½ tablespoon olive oil

2 teaspoons chopped fresh thyme, divided

2 garlic cloves, crushed

1 cup red, orange, yellow, and green bell peppers, cut into 1½-inch strips

2 tablespoons fresh flat-leaf parsley leaves

Preheat the oven to 425°F.

TO MAKE THE PORK

1. Heat the olive oil in a large ovenproof skillet over medium-high heat, swirling to coat. Sprinkle the pork with ½ teaspoon of pepper and ⅛ teaspoon of salt. Add the pork to the skillet and cook for about 4 minutes. Turn the pork over and cook 1 minute more.

2. Cover the skillet with aluminum foil and bake for 10 minutes. Remove and discard the foil. Bake the pork for an additional 5 minutes, or until an instant-read thermometer registers 145°F. Transfer the pork to a cutting board and let it rest for about 10 minutes; do not turn the oven off. Cut the pork across the grain into slices.

3. Return the skillet to medium-high heat. In a small bowl, whisk together the remaining ½ teaspoon of pepper and ⅛ teaspoon of salt, the stock, cornstarch, and vinegar. Add the stock mixture to the skillet, bring to a boil, and cook for about 2 minutes, or until the sauce has slightly thickened. Transfer the sauce to a bowl and keep it warm.

**TO MAKE THE PEPPERS**

1.  In the same skillet over medium-high heat, add the olive oil and swirl to coat. Add 1 teaspoon of thyme, the garlic, and bell peppers and cook, stirring frequently, for 1½ minutes.

2.  Divide the pork and bell pepper mixture between two serving plates; sprinkle with the remaining 1 teaspoon of thyme and the parsley. Drizzle with the sauce and serve.

*Perfectly Portioned Plate:* Serve this dish with a spinach and mushroom salad and wild rice.

**Per Serving:** Calories: 269; Fats: 12g; Protein: 32g; Cholesterol: 83mg; Carbohydrates: 10g; Fiber: 2g; Sodium: 342mg

# Pork Medallions with Mustard Sauce

**DAIRY-FREE, QUICK & EASY / PREP TIME: 5 MINUTES / COOK TIME: 10 MINUTES**

This simple one-pan pork dish made with a few basic pantry ingredients makes it easy to have a nutritious dinner on the table in no time. While the word "mustard" used in conjunction with pork may conjure up not-so-healthy images of ballparks, mustard, like all herbs and spices, is rich in vitamins, minerals, and health-promoting phytochemicals. A member of the cruciferous vegetable family, mustard seed contains high levels of the antioxidant mineral selenium and is a good source of the mineral magnesium, important for a healthy blood pressure.

8 ounces pork tenderloin, cut crosswise into 4 slices

⅛ teaspoon salt

¼ teaspoon freshly ground black pepper

1 tablespoon olive oil, divided

1 tablespoon Dijon mustard

¼ cup low-sodium chicken stock

1 teaspoon oat flour

1. Gently flatten the pork slices using the palm of your hand. Sprinkle with the salt and pepper.

2. Heat ½ tablespoon of olive oil in a large skillet over medium-high heat and swirl to coat. Add the pork to the skillet and cook for about 3 minutes on each side, or until an instant-read thermometer registers 145°F. Remove the pork from the skillet and keep it warm.

3. Add the mustard and the remaining ½ tablespoon of olive oil to the skillet, stirring until combined. Whisk in the stock and flour. Bring to a boil and cook for about 1 minute, or until the mixture thickens, scraping the bottom of the pan to loosen any brown bits. Spoon the sauce over the pork and serve.

*Perfectly Portioned Plate:* Serve this dish with a fresh salad of mixed baby greens and a side of steamed asparagus and baby red potatoes.

**Per Serving:** Calories: 233; Fats: 11g; Protein: 30g; Cholesterol: 83g; Carbohyddrates: 1g; Fiber: 0g; Sodium: 396mg

# Pork and Asparagus Stir-Fry

**DAIRY-FREE, QUICK & EASY / PREP TIME: 10 MINUTES / COOK TIME: 10 MINUTES**

Stir-fry dishes are an excellent way to boost your intake of nutritious vegetables and dietary fiber, plus they are easy to prep and cook in a matter of minutes. In this recipe, lean, protein-rich pork tenderloin strips are quickly stir-fried with asparagus, which offers folate and fiber, and colorful red bell peppers, an abundant source of vitamin C. The rice wine (sake) adds a slightly sweet taste to this flavorful dish.

2 teaspoons low-sodium soy sauce, divided

2½ teaspoons cornstarch, divided

2 teaspoons sake (rice wine) or dry sherry

1 teaspoon cider vinegar

2 teaspoons sesame oil

8 ounces pork tenderloin, trimmed and cut into strips

⅓ cup unsalted chicken stock

½ tablespoon olive oil

4 garlic cloves, minced

1 tablespoon peeled and minced fresh ginger

1 cup (2-inch pieces) red bell pepper

½ cup chopped onion

½ cup snow peas

8 ounces asparagus, trimmed and cut into 2-inch pieces

1. In a large bowl, whisk together 1 teaspoon of soy sauce, 2 teaspoons of cornstarch, the sake, cider vinegar, and sesame oil. Add the pork and toss to coat. Set it aside.

2. In a small bowl, stir together the remaining 1 teaspoon of soy sauce, ½ teaspoon of cornstarch, and the stock. Set it aside.

3. Heat a wok or large skillet over high heat. Add the olive oil, swirling to coat. Add the garlic and ginger and stir-fry for 30 seconds, or until fragrant. Add the pork mixture to the wok and stir-fry for about 3 minutes, or until browned. Add the bell pepper, onion, snow peas, and asparagus and stir-fry for about 3 minutes, or until crisp-tender. Add the stock mixture, bring to a boil, and cook for 2 minutes, or until the sauce has slightly thickened.

4. Serve immediately.

*Perfectly Portioned Plate:* Serve this stir-fry over brown rice with a side salad of mixed baby greens, carrots, tomatoes, and mushrooms.

**Per Serving:** Calories: 342; Fats: 13g; Protein: 36g; Cholesterol: 83mg; Carbohydrates: 22g; Fiber: 6g; Sodium: 468mg

# Steak Skewers with Strawberry Chimichurri

DAIRY-FREE, GLUTEN-FREE, QUICK & EASY / PREP TIME: 10 MINUTES / COOK TIME: 10 MINUTES

Red meat is a food you should include sparingly in your heart healthy diet. Think of it as a monthly treat, rather than a weekly menu item. Red meat is an excellent source of complete, high-quality protein and is rich in iron and other essential vitamins and minerals, but the cut you choose makes all the difference in terms of saturated fat content. This recipe uses skirt steak, a lean cut that makes a great choice for skewers and fajitas. Chimichurri sauce, boosting the fiber content of the entrée, is made using vitamin C–rich strawberries for a steak recipe you can feel good about including in your diet.

¾ cup finely diced strawberries

½ cup chopped fresh parsley

3 teaspoons chopped
    fresh oregano

1 teaspoon chopped
    fresh thyme

2 tablespoons minced shallot

2 tablespoons olive oil

2 tablespoons red wine vinegar

2 teaspoons honey

⅛ teaspoon salt

½ teaspoon freshly ground
    black pepper, divided

8 ounces skirt steak, trimmed

1 teaspoon ground cumin

¼ teaspoon cayenne pepper

½ tablespoon chili powder

Olive oil nonstick cooking spray

1. In a medium bowl, gently mix together the strawberries, parsley, oregano, thyme, shallot, olive oil, vinegar, honey, salt, and ¼ teaspoon of pepper. Set it aside.

2. Cut the steak crosswise into two equal pieces then cut each piece lengthwise into four 1-inch-wide strips. Place the strips in a large bowl. Add the cumin, cayenne, chili powder, and remaining ¼ teaspoon of pepper and toss well to coat. Thread the strips onto four metal skewers.

3. Lightly coat a grill with cooking spray or line it with aluminum foil and then heat to very high. Place the skewers on the grill and cook for 3 to 5 minutes per side or to your desired degree of doneness, depending on the thickness of the skirt steak. Transfer to a cutting board and let them rest.

4. Serve with the strawberry chimichurri sauce.

*Perfectly Portioned Plate:* Serve the skewers with a fresh salad of mixed baby greens, chopped tomatoes and mushrooms, and a side of steamed broccoli.

**Per Serving:** Calories: 420; Fats: 21g; Protein: 43g; Cholesterol: 102mg; Carbohydrates: 16g; Fiber: 4g; Sodium: 231mg

# Steak with Onions and Peppers

DAIRY-FREE, GLUTEN-FREE, QUICK & EASY / PREP TIME: 5 MINUTES / COOK TIME: 12 MINUTES

This simple steak dinner recipe uses lean top round steak to keep saturated fat in check, and balances out the entrée with generous portions of onions, bell peppers, and mushrooms, which provide fiber, vitamin C, vitamin D, and phytochemicals. With the cholesterol-lowering phyto-chemical *allicin* from the garlic, the vegetable mix is a perfect complement to the steak, adding lots of flavor without added fat. Have all of your vegetables sliced and ready before you start cooking as this recipe takes only minutes to prepare.

8 ounces top round steak,
    cut into thin strips
Salt
Freshly ground black pepper
Olive oil nonstick
    cooking spray
½ large white onion,
    cut into rings
1 small green bell pepper,
    cut into big chunks
1 small red bell pepper,
    cut into big chunks
2 teaspoons crushed garlic
½ teaspoon olive oil
½ cup sliced mushrooms

1. Season steak with salt and pepper.

2. Heat a large skillet over high heat and spray it with cooking spray.

3. Add half the steak, cook for 1 minute, turn the strips over, and cook for 30 seconds more. Transfer the strips to a large dish.

4. Spray the skillet with cooking spray again. Add the remaining steak, cook for 1 minute, turn the strips over, and cook for 30 seconds more. Add to the dish with the cooked steak strips.

5. Return the skillet to the heat and spray with cooking spray again. Add the onion, bell peppers, and garlic and season with salt and pepper. Cook for 3 to 4 minutes, or until the onions are golden and the peppers are soft. Add the cooked vegetables to the dish with the steak.

6. Decrease the heat to medium and add the olive oil to the skillet. Add the mushrooms and cook for about 4 minutes.

7. Add the mushrooms to the dish with the steak, onions, and peppers and stir to combine. Serve immediately.

*Perfectly Portioned Plate:* Serve the steak and vegetables over brown rice with a salad of mixed baby greens and sliced tomatoes.

**Per Serving:** Calories: 285; Fats: 7g; Protein: 43g; Cholesterol: 102mg; Carbohydrates: 11g; Fiber: 3g; Sodium: 134mg

# Grilled Tip Sirloin Steak with Mango Salsa

**DAIRY-FREE, GLUTEN-FREE, QUICK & EASY / PREP TIME: 5 MINUTES / COOK TIME: 15 MINUTES**

Steak is an excellent source of iron, protein, and B vitamins, but it needs a little help to make a well-rounded meal. Adding a fresh mango salsa is a great way to add dietary fiber, phytochemicals, vitamins A and C, plus other nutrients while adding a lively flavor. Mangos are an especially heart healthy choice because they are rich in a type of dietary fiber called pectin, important for lowering bad cholesterol (LDL). Rich in potassium and magnesium, this "king of fruits" can also help maintain a healthy blood pressure. So double the salsa recipe to use on tomorrow's lunch.

2 (4-ounce) sirloin steaks

⅛ teaspoon salt, plus more for seasoning

½ teaspoon freshly ground black pepper, plus more for seasoning

Nonstick olive oil cooking spray

1 red bell pepper, sliced

1 mango, halved, peeled, and seeded

½ white onion, sliced

1 tomato, halved

1 tablespoon freshly squeezed lime juice

½ teaspoon apple cider vinegar

¼ cup chopped fresh cilantro

1. Prepare a grill for direct-heat cooking over hot charcoal (high heat for gas).

2. Pat the steaks dry and season them with salt and pepper.

3. Oil the grill rack and place the steak, bell pepper, mango, onion, and tomato on the grill.

4. Grill the vegetables and mango for 2 to 3 minutes. Transfer to a cutting board and dice. Place in a small bowl.

5. Turn the steaks occasionally and grill for 6 to 8 minutes for medium (140°F) or 8 to 10 minutes for medium-well (150°F). Transfer the steaks to two serving plates to rest.

6. Meanwhile, stir the lime juice, vinegar, and cilantro into the grilled mango mixture.

7. Season the salsa with ⅛ teaspoon of salt and ½ teaspoon of pepper and serve over the steaks.

*Perfectly Portioned Plate:* Serve with steamed yellow squash and zucchini and a salad of mixed baby greens.

**Per Serving:** Calories: 349; Fats: 8g; Protein: 37g; Cholesterol: 101mg; Carbohydrates: 34g; Fiber: 5g; Sodium: 229mg

# Red Onions Stuffed with Grilled Steak and Spinach

DAIRY-FREE, GLUTEN-FREE / PREP TIME: 10 MINUTES / COOK TIME: 55 MINUTES

This creative recipe uses flavorful red onions stuffed with lean flank steak seasoned with ginger and the bold Indian spice garam masala. Spinach and golden raisins boost the fiber, vitamin, mineral, and phytochemical content for a dish that is as impressive to serve as it is delicious to eat. This dish can be made in advance and refrigerated for up to one day before cooking. Unique and full of nutrients, this fragrant recipe makes a nice change of pace from stuffed peppers.

2 (15- to 16-ounce) red onions, peeled and tops removed

1 tablespoon olive oil

2 teaspoons minced garlic

2 teaspoons minced fresh ginger

½ teaspoon garam masala

½ teaspoon ground cumin

2 tablespoons golden raisins

2 tablespoons water

8 ounces grilled flank steak, cut into ½-inch dice

8 ounces baby spinach, roughly chopped

½ tablespoon freshly squeezed lemon juice

Salt

Freshly ground black pepper

1. In a 4-quart pot, bring 2 quarts of water to a boil. Carefully place the onions in the boiling water and cook for 25 to 30 minutes, or until they are tender but still retain their shape. Drain and let them cool.

2. Position a rack in the center of the oven and preheat the oven to 375°F.

3. When the onions are cool enough to handle, cut them in half crosswise and trim the root ends. Holding an onion wrapped in a clean towel, use your fingers to carefully remove the core from each half of the onion, leaving a ½-inch thick shell. Cut a small amount off the bottom of each half so they sit upright. Repeat with the second onion. Roughly chop and reserve ½ cup of the removed onion core.

*continued »*

4.  In a large skillet over medium-high heat, heat the olive oil until it shimmers. Add the garlic and ginger and cook, stirring, for about 1½ minutes, or until lightly browned. Add the garam masala and cumin and continue cooking, stirring, for about 30 seconds, or until fragrant. Decrease the heat to medium, add the raisins and water and cook for about 1 minute, or until the raisins are plump. Add the reserved chopped onion and the flank steak and cook, stirring frequently, 1 to 2 minutes, or until heated through. Add the spinach and cook, stirring, for 1 to 2 minutes, or until wilted. Add the lemon juice and season with salt and pepper.

5.  Spoon the filling into the onion halves, mounding it slightly. Put the onions on a rimmed baking sheet and bake until the tops just begin to brown, about 15 minutes. Serve immediately.

*Perfectly Portioned Plate:* Serve this dish with a Greek salad and quinoa with a tablespoon of raisins mixed in.

**Per Serving:** Calories: 521; Fats: 14g; Protein: 50g; Cholesterol: 102mg; Carbohydrates: 53g; Fiber: 12g; Sodium: 238mg

# Pork Chops with Tomato and Fennel Sauce

DAIRY-FREE, GLUTEN-FREE, QUICK & EASY / PREP TIME: 10 MINUTES / COOK TIME: 20 MINUTES

With a distinctive licorice flavor, fennel pairs naturally with pork and tomatoes in this bright, tasty dish. Fennel's fiber, potassium, folate, vitamin C, vitamin $B_6$, and phytonutrient content all support heart health by lowering cholesterol, reducing inflammation, and keeping homocysteine levels in check. Paired with tomatoes rich in lycopene—a powerful and protective phytochemical—this dish can be prepared in just half an hour.

2 teaspoons olive oil

1 fennel bulb, thinly sliced
    (2 to 3 cups)

2 medium shallots, thinly sliced

3 garlic cloves, minced

1 (14-ounce) can diced
    tomatoes, with juices

¾ teaspoon dried oregano

½ teaspoon dried rosemary

¼ teaspoon dried thyme

Salt

Freshly ground black pepper

1 garlic clove, peeled and
    halved lengthwise

4 (2-ounce) boneless,
    center-cut pork chops
    (about ¼-inch thick)

¼ cup chopped fresh parsley

1. In a large nonstick skillet over medium-high heat, add the olive oil, fennel, and shallots and sauté for 4 to 5 minutes.

2. Add the garlic and cook for an additional minute. Add the tomatoes, oregano, rosemary, and thyme and season with salt and pepper. Simmer for 8 to 10 minutes.

3. About 5 minutes into the simmering time, take the garlic clove and rub both sides of the pork chops. Season the chops with salt and pepper. Cook the chops in the skillet for 3 to 4 minutes per side until an instant-read thermometer registers 145°F. Allow them to rest for 1 minute.

4. Divide the tomato-fennel mixture between two serving plates and top each with 2 pork chops. Garnish with the fresh parsley and enjoy immediately.

*Perfectly Portioned Plate:* Serve with a side of steamed broccoli, zucchini, and yellow squash.

**Per Serving:** Calories: 497; Fats: 28g; Protein: 30g; Cholesterol: 98mg; Carbohydrates: 21g; Fiber: 7g; Sodium: 312mg

Cauliflower Salad with Cherry Tomatoes, p. 171

# 9

# Sides

# Homemade Hash Browns

**DAIRY-FREE, GLUTEN-FREE, VEGAN, QUICK & EASY / PREP TIME: 10 MINUTES
COOK TIME: 20 MINUTES**

These homemade hash brown patties get a fiber, vitamin, and mineral boost with the addition of finely chopped vegetables. Sweet potato, rich in beta-carotene and phytochemicals, adds a creative twist—and flavor—to the more traditional white potato. Spinach and carrots add B vitamins, vitamin C, fiber, antioxidants, and more phytochemicals to create a filling, versatile side dish that is easy to customize using vegetables that you have on hand.

1 sweet potato, peeled
   and grated

1 Yukon gold potato, peeled
   and grated

½ cup chopped spinach leaves

¼ cup finely chopped onion

¼ cup grated carrots

⅛ teaspoon salt

1½ tablespoons gluten-free
   oat flour

Pinch freshly ground
   black pepper

2 teaspoons olive oil

1. In a medium bowl, mix together the sweet potato, gold potato, spinach, onion, and carrots. Add the salt and mix well.

2. Using your hands, squeeze the veggie mixture to remove all the moisture. Sprinkle in the oat flour and a pinch of pepper and mix to combine. Divide the potato mixture into four mounds and form each mound into patties.

3. Heat the olive oil in a large skillet over medium-high heat. Add the patties, press down gently, and brown for 4 to 5 minutes. Decrease the heat to medium and cook for 5 minutes more. Flip the patties and continue to cook 5 to 10 more minutes, or until crispy and brown. Serve warm.

*Perfectly Portioned Plate:* Serve these hash browns with Tofu Kale Scramble (page 99).

**Per Serving:** Calories: 226; Fats: 5g; Protein: 5g; Cholesterol: 0mg; Carbohydrates: 42g; Fiber: 6g; Sodium: 204mg

# Roasted Brussels Sprouts

**DAIRY-FREE, GLUTEN-FREE, VEGAN, QUICK & EASY / PREP TIME: 5 MINUTES / COOK TIME: 12 MINUTES**

They might be small, but Brussels sprouts are nutritional powerhouses and roasting them brings out their wonderful nuttiness. Unfortunately, many people have unpleasant childhood memories associated with Brussels sprouts, a vegetable voted most-hated in both the United States and Britain. You can avoid childhood flashbacks and preserve flavor and nutrients by not overcooking them. Low in calories and high in vitamin C, B vitamins, potassium, antioxidants, and fiber, this veggie can help keep cholesterol levels in check. This recipe uses a simple seasoning to complement the sprouts without overwhelming them.

1 cup Brussels sprouts

1 teaspoon olive oil

1 teaspoon balsamic vinegar

Salt

Freshly ground black pepper

1. Preheat the oven to 450°F and line a baking sheet with aluminum foil.

2. Trim the ends of the Brussels sprouts and remove any bruised outer leaves. Halve the sprouts and place them on the prepared baking sheet. Add the olive oil and vinegar and season with salt and pepper. Using your hands, mix them together to coat. Spread the sprouts out in a single layer, being careful not to over-crowd them.

3. Bake for 10 to 12 minutes, stirring them halfway through. Serve warm.

*Perfectly Portioned Plate:* Serve this side with Lentil Walnut Burgers (page 107).

**Per Serving:** Calories: 40; Fats: 3g; Protein: 2g; Cholesterol: 0mg; Carbohydrates: 4g; Fiber: 2g; Sodium: 89mg

# Cauliflower Mashed "Potatoes"

GLUTEN-FREE, QUICK & EASY / PREP TIME: 5 MINUTES / COOK TIME: 8 MINUTES

Cauliflower is one of the most versatile and nutritious vegetables there is. Easy to transform into a perfect pizza crust and a tasty fried rice, it's also a delicious and fiber-rich alternative to mashed potatoes. Cauliflower is a member of the cruciferous vegetable family and you will want to include it in your diet on a regular basis to reap all of its health benefits. A one-cup serving has almost 75 percent of your RDA for vitamin C as well as numerous antioxidant phytonutrients. Feel free to vary the spices in this recipe to those you usually use for your mashed potatoes.

1½-pound head of cauliflower, chopped into florets
3 garlic cloves, chopped
1 teaspoon fresh thyme
1 teaspoon chopped fresh chives
1 teaspoon olive oil
2 tablespoons nonfat milk or plant-based milk
Pinch salt
Pinch freshly ground black pepper

1. Fill a large saucepan with about 1 inch of water and insert a steamer basket. Bring the water to a boil and add the cauliflower florets to the basket. Decrease the heat to a simmer and cover, allowing the cauliflower to steam for 6 to 8 minutes, or until fork-tender.

2. Drain the steamed cauliflower and transfer it to the bowl of a large food processor. Add the garlic, thyme, chives, olive oil, milk, salt, and pepper, and process to your desired texture. Serve warm.

*Perfectly Portioned Plate:* Serve these with Pan-Roasted Pork Tenderloin and Peppers (page 146).

**Per Serving:** Calories: 119; Fats: 3g; Protein: 8g; Cholesterol: 0mg; Carbohydrates: 21g; Fiber: 9g; Sodium: 189mg

# Oven-Roasted Garlic Cabbage

DAIRY-FREE, GLUTEN-FREE, VEGAN / PREP TIME: 5 MINUTES / COOK TIME: 40 MINUTES

This satisfying recipe for oven-roasted garlic cabbage is a healthy and creative spin on calorie-laden garlic bread. Cabbage is an excellent source of the antioxidant vitamin C, vitamin $B_6$ (which is needed to keep homocysteine levels in check), and a very good source of fiber, potassium, and phytochemicals shown to suppress the inflammation that may lead to cardiovascular disease. Quick to prepare, this pairs nicely with Italian cuisines but works with just about any dish as a healthy, nutritious side.

½ head of cabbage, cut into 1-inch-thick slices
1 tablespoon olive oil
3 garlic cloves, minced
1 tablespoon dried chives
Salt
Freshly ground black pepper

1. Preheat the oven to 400°F.

2. Brush both sides of the cabbage slices with the olive oil.

3. Pat the garlic evenly onto each side of the cabbage slices. Sprinkle each side with chives then season them with salt and pepper. Lay the slices on a baking sheet.

4. Roast for 20 minutes, turn the slices over, and roast for another 20 minutes, or until the edges are crispy. Serve immediately.

*Perfectly Portioned Plate:* Serve this side with Rainbow Trout Baked in Foil with Tomatoes and Thyme (page 132).

**Per Serving:** Calories: 117; Fats: 7g; Protein: 3g; Cholesterol: 0mg; Carbohydrates: 13g; Fiber: 5g; Sodium: 114mg

# Oven-Roasted Sweet Potato Fries

DAIRY-FREE, GLUTEN-FREE, VEGAN / PREP TIME: 5 MINUTES / COOK TIME: 30 MINUTES

Simple, healthy, fast, and packed with flavor, baked sweet potato fries make a great snack or side dish that will fill you up and keep you energized. Sweet potatoes pack a nutritional punch—one medium-size potato contains over twice the amount of vitamin A you need for the day in addition to inflammation-reducing phytochemicals, complex carbohydrates, and fiber. You can change things up a bit by adjusting the seasonings.

2 sweet potatoes, scrubbed

1 tablespoon olive oil

1 teaspoon garlic powder

1 teaspoon paprika

¼ teaspoon freshly ground
    black pepper

⅛ teaspoon cayenne pepper

⅛ teaspoon salt

1. Preheat the oven to 425°F.

2. Leaving the skins on and using a very sharp knife, cut the sweet potatoes into thin, even matchsticks.

3. Transfer the matchsticks to a large baking sheet and drizzle with the olive oil. Sprinkle with the garlic powder, paprika, black pepper, cayenne pepper, and salt and toss to coat. Arrange the potatoes in a single layer to ensure they crisp up.

4. Bake for 15 minutes and flip to cook the other side. Bake for an additional 10 to 15 minutes, or until crispy and brown. Serve immediately.

*Perfectly Portioned Plate:* Serve these oven fries with Grilled Chicken Breasts with Plum Salsa (page 128).

**Per Serving:** Calories: 334; Fats: 8g; Protein: 4g; Cholesterol: 0mg; Carbohydrates: 65g; Fiber: 10g; Sodium: 168mg

# Asparagus "Fries"

**DAIRY-FREE, VEGAN, QUICK & EASY / PREP TIME: 15 MINUTES / COOK TIME: 15 MINUTES**

Eating more vegetables can be as easy as finding creative ways to use them to replace your favorite higher-calorie, less-healthy foods. Asparagus is loaded with heart healthy benefits including high levels of dietary fiber, vitamins and minerals, and asparagine—an amino acid that acts as a natural diuretic, which is beneficial for those with high blood pressure. To make a suitable "fry" replacement, the asparagus is coated in bread crumbs, resulting in a crisp, crunchy, healthy French fry substitute that is certain to hit the spot.

½ bunch asparagus, ends trimmed and spears cut in half

1 tablespoon ground flaxseed mixed with 3 tablespoons water, or 1 beaten egg

¼ cup bread crumbs

1 teaspoon mustard powder

½ teaspoon garlic powder

⅛ teaspoon salt

1. Preheat the oven to 400°F and line a baking sheet with parchment or a silicone baking mat.

2. Mix the ground flaxseed with the water (or egg) and allow it to sit for 5 minutes.

3. In a shallow bowl, combine the bread crumbs, mustard powder, garlic powder, and salt.

4. Dip each asparagus length into the flaxseed and water and then into the bread crumb mixture, then place them on the prepared baking sheet, being careful not to overcrowd them.

5. Bake for 15 minutes, or until crispy and browned. Serve immediately.

*Perfectly Portioned Plate:* Serve this side with Lemon Garlic Mackerel (page 137).

**Per Serving:** Calories: 119; Fats: 4g; Protein: 8g; Cholesterol: 82mg; Carbohydrates: 16g; Fiber: 3g; Sodium: 280mg

# Vegetable Kabobs

DAIRY-FREE, GLUTEN-FREE, VEGAN / PREP TIME: 25 MINUTES / COOK TIME: 12 MINUTES

Nothing meets the recommendation to "eat the rainbow" better than preparing a colorful mixed vegetable kabob. This recipe uses a simple yet flavorful garlic marinade to bring out even more flavor in the roasted vegetables. Go ahead and omit or replace any of the vegetables here with your favorites or whatever is in season. These kabobs can also be cooked on an outdoor grill. Colorful and full of fiber, vitamins, and minerals, these tasty kabobs make a satisfying side dish for any entrée.

2 tablespoons olive oil
2 garlic cloves, crushed
Juice of ½ lemon
½ teaspoon dried oregano
½ teaspoon dried basil
Salt
Freshly ground black pepper
1 cup cremini mushrooms
½ cup cherry tomatoes
1 green bell pepper,
    cut into chunks
1 red onion, cut into chunks
1 yellow squash, cut into
    thick rounds

1. Preheat the oven to 400°F.

2. In a small bowl, whisk together the olive oil, garlic, lemon juice, oregano, and basil. Season with salt and pepper.

3. Thread the mushrooms, tomatoes, bell pepper, onion, and squash onto skewers. Place the skewers on a baking sheet. Brush the vegetables with the oil mixture and let them sit for 10 to 15 minutes.

4. Roast for 10 to 12 minutes, or until tender, and serve immediately.

*Perfectly Portioned Plate:* Serve these skewers with Broiled Tuna Steaks with Peppercorn-Lime Rub (page 138).

**Per Serving:** Calories: 191; Fats: 15g; Protein: 4g; Cholesterol: 0mg; Carbohydrates: 15g; Fiber: 4g; Sodium: 96mg

# Sesame Steamed Summer Squash

**DAIRY-FREE, VEGAN, QUICK & EASY / PREP TIME: 5 MINUTES / COOK TIME: 8 MINUTES**

This recipe is a simple way to dress up nutrient-rich summer squash that doesn't require much time and uses basic pantry ingredients. A dash of low-sodium soy sauce and a sprinkle of sesame seeds is all that is needed to give this dish a crunchy Asian flair. Zucchini and yellow squash are very low in calories yet high in fiber, vitamins, and minerals, and can add filling volume to your meals to help you feel satisfied with fewer calories.

1 small zucchini

1 small yellow squash

1 tablespoon freshly squeezed lemon juice

1 teaspoon sesame oil

1 teaspoon low-sodium soy sauce

1 garlic clove, minced

2 teaspoons sesame seeds

Pinch salt

Pinch freshly ground black pepper

1. Add 1 inch of water to a small saucepan and place a steamer basket inside. Bring the water to a boil. Cut the zucchini and yellow squash in half lengthwise and then into ½-inch slices. Add the zucchini and yellow squash slices to the steamer basket, cover, and steam for 5 to 7 minutes, or until tender.

2. Meanwhile, in a small bowl, whisk together the lemon juice, sesame oil, soy sauce, garlic, sesame seeds, salt, and pepper.

3. Transfer the squash to a serving bowl, drizzle with the dressing, and toss to coat. Serve immediately.

*Perfectly Portioned Plate:* Serve this dish with Asian Chicken Lettuce Wraps (page 124).

**Per Serving:** Calories: 74; Fats: 4g; Protein: 3g; Cholesterol: 0mg; Carbohydrates: 8g; Fiber: 3g; Sodium: 171mg

# Green Bean and Edamame Succotash

DAIRY-FREE, GLUTEN-FREE, VEGAN, QUICK & EASY / PREP TIME: 5 MINUTES / COOK TIME: 9 MINUTES

This recipe swaps out lima beans for edamame to make a variation on the traditional succotash. Edamame are high in complete high-quality soy protein and are rich in cholesterol-lowering fiber, making them a good addition to a heart healthy diet. Fresh basil adds a pungent flavor and a sweet earthy aroma while adding an impressive list of nutrients, including the antioxidant vitamin C and B vitamins that are so important for heart health.

½ cup green beans, trimmed

1 teaspoon olive oil

¼ cup corn kernels (fresh or frozen and thawed)

½ cup frozen shelled edamame, thawed

¼ cup chopped red bell pepper

¼ cup chopped red onion

¼ cup chopped fresh basil

Salt

Freshly ground black pepper

1. Add 1 inch of water to a small saucepan and place a steamer basket inside. Bring the water to a boil. Add the green beans to the steamer basket, cover, and steam for 4 minutes, or until crisp tender.

2. Heat the olive oil in a medium skillet over medium-high heat. Add the green beans and sauté for 1 minute. Add the corn, edamame, bell pepper, and onion and sauté for about 4 minutes, or until the vegetables are tender.

3. Transfer to a mixing bowl, add the basil, and season with salt and pepper. Serve immediately.

*Perfectly Portioned Plate:* Serve this dish with grilled or baked fish or poultry.

**Per Serving:** Calories: 150; Fats: 7g; Protein: 10g; Cholesterol: 0mg; Carbohydrates: 15g; Fiber: 5g; Sodium: 93mg

# Sautéed Kale with Blood Orange Dressing

**DAIRY-FREE, GLUTEN-FREE, QUICK & EASY / PREP TIME: 5 MINUTES / COOK TIME: 8 MINUTES**

This simple, refreshing recipe uses vitamin C–rich blood oranges to create a flavorful and nutritious dressing for lightly sautéed kale. Blood oranges are named for their deep red flesh, which is due to anthocyanin, an antioxidant found in many red fruits and vegetables that can reduce the risk of coronary heart disease. With a distinctively different flavor from navel oranges, blood oranges are less acidic in taste, with overtones of berries that make them a delightful addition to savory dishes.

2 blood oranges (1 halved, 1 peeled and segmented)
2 tablespoons olive oil, plus 1 teaspoon
1 teaspoon honey
1 bunch kale, stems removed and chopped
¼ cup chopped walnuts
Freshly ground black pepper

1.  Squeeze 3 tablespoons of juice from the halved blood orange. In a small bowl, mix together the orange juice, 2 tablespoons of olive oil, and the honey. Set it aside.

2.  In a medium skillet, heat the remaining 1 teaspoon of olive oil, add the chopped kale stems and centers and sauté for 3 to 4 minutes, or until softened.

3.  Add the kale leaves to the skillet, pour half of the dressing over them, and sauté for 2 to 3 minutes, or until the leaves are wilted and tender. Add the orange segments and cook for 1 minute, or until warm. Remove from the heat and add the remaining dressing, tossing lightly to combine.

4.  Serve the kale topped with the walnuts and seasoned with pepper.

*Perfectly Portioned Plate:* Serve this dish with Salmon and Summer Squash in Parchment (page 130).

**Per Serving:** Calories: 433; Fats: 26g; Protein: 12g; Cholesterol: 0mg; Carbohydrates: 47g; Fiber: 9g; Sodium: 87mg

# Roasted Romaine Lettuce

DAIRY-FREE, GLUTEN-FREE, VEGAN, QUICK & EASY / PREP TIME: 1 MINUTE / COOK TIME: 10 MINUTES

Romaine lettuce takes on a nice charred flavor when roasted or grilled. One of the most nutritious varieties of salad green, romaine's vitamin C and beta-carotene content makes it a heart healthy green as these nutrients work together to prevent the buildup of cholesterol in artery walls. The fiber, folic acid, and potassium content in romaine lettuce add even more heart healthy benefits by keeping homocysteine levels in check and lowering blood pressure. In this recipe, a simple dressing allows romaine's natural sweetness to shine.

1 head romaine lettuce
1 tablespoon olive oil
Salt
Freshly ground black pepper
1 Persian cucumber, diced
½ cup halved cherry tomatoes

1. Preheat the broiler.

2. Cut the romaine in half lengthwise. Drizzle the olive oil on the cut sides and season with salt and pepper.

3. Place the halves on a baking sheet and broil for 3 to 5 minutes on each side, or until the desired char is reached.

4. Transfer the lettuce to serving plates, top with the cucumber and tomatoes, and serve immediately.

*Perfectly Portioned Plate:* Serve this dish alongside grilled fish or chicken.

**Per Serving:** Calories: 113; Fats: 8g; Protein: 2g; Cholesterol: 0mg; Carbohydrates: 12g; Fiber: 2g; Sodium: 92mg

# Sage-Roasted Baby Carrots

DAIRY-FREE, GLUTEN-FREE, VEGAN, QUICK & EASY / PREP TIME: 5 MINUTES / COOK TIME: 20 MINUTES

In less than half an hour you can have a delicious and nutritious side dish that will really stand out on your plate. Citric acid from the lemon helps soften the carrots, and sage adds a soft yet sweet savory flavor along with numerous beneficial antioxidant and anti-inflammatory compounds. Roasted with heart healthy olive oil, the light and zingy taste of the carrots makes them a perfect accompaniment to grilled meats, fish, and cooked beans.

1 pound baby carrots

2 tablespoons chopped fresh sage

1 tablespoon orange zest

1 tablespoon olive oil

Juice of ½ lemon

1. Preheat the oven to 425°F and line a baking sheet with parchment paper.

2. In a medium bowl, combine the carrots, sage, orange zest, and olive oil.

3. Spread the carrots in a single layer on the prepared baking sheet and roast for about 20 minutes, or until soft and slightly browned.

4. Drizzle the lemon juice over the carrots before serving.

*Perfectly Portioned Plate:* Serve this dish with Sesame-Crusted Tuna Steaks (page 134).

**Per Serving:** Calories: 149; Fats: 7g; Protein: 2g; Cholesterol: 0g; Carbohydrates: 21g; Fiber: 8g; Sodium: 177mg

# Steamed Broccoli Mash

**GLUTEN-FREE, QUICK & EASY / PREP TIME: 5 MINUTES / COOK TIME: 15 MINUTES**

This is a great recipe for making use of the entire broccoli vegetable: florets, stalks, and stems. It also works well with frozen broccoli, and broccoli that is just past its prime. Broccoli is such a nutritious vegetable and is one that you should aim to include in your diet several times a week in order to meet cruciferous intake recommendations for health and disease prevention. Greek yogurt helps make the mash extra creamy, but go ahead and substitute it with nondairy yogurt, light coconut milk, or a plant-based milk instead.

1 head of broccoli, florets
and stems
1 teaspoon olive oil
2 garlic cloves, minced
¼ cup nonfat plain
Greek yogurt
Salt
Freshly ground black pepper

1. Add 1 inch of water to a saucepan and place a steamer basket inside. Bring the water to a boil. Add the broccoli to the steamer basket and steam for about 5 minutes, or until tender.

2. Add the broccoli, olive oil, garlic, and Greek yogurt to the bowl of a food processor. Season with salt and pepper and purée on high until the broccoli mash reaches your desired consistency. Serve immediately.

*Perfectly Portioned Plate:* Serve the broccoli mash with Steak with Onions and Peppers (page 151).

**Per Serving:** Calories: 108; Fats: 3g; Protein: 7g; Cholesterol: 2mg; Carbohydrates: 15g; Fiber: 5g; Sodium: 159mg

# Cauliflower Salad with Cherry Tomatoes

DAIRY-FREE, GLUTEN-FREE, VEGAN / PREP TIME: 10 MINUTES / COOK TIME: 30 MINUTES

Sheet pan side dishes are great time savers during the week when you don't have the time to do a lot of cooking. Prep and clean up are relatively easy and you can make a double batch and have leftovers for later. This simple, nutrient-rich dish couldn't be easier. Just toss together some tomatoes, cauliflower, and Swiss chard—three foods packed with inflammation-reducing phytochemicals, antioxidants, and cholesterol-lowering fiber—drizzle them with heart healthy olive oil, and roast them to bring out their natural sweet flavors.

2 cups cauliflower florets, thinly sliced
1 cup halved cherry tomatoes
1 bunch Swiss chard
1 tablespoon olive oil
½ teaspoon capers
¼ teaspoon red chili flakes
Salt
Freshly ground black pepper
½ lemon

1. Preheat the oven to 450°F.

2. In a large bowl, add the cauliflower, tomatoes, Swiss chard, olive oil, capers, and chili flakes. Season with salt and pepper and toss to combine.

3. Line a baking sheet with parchment paper and spread the vegetables out on the sheet. Cook for 25 to 30 minutes, stirring occasionally. The tomatoes should start to release their juices, the cauliflower should start to turn golden brown, and the Swiss chard should wilt.

4. Remove from the oven and serve topped with a squeeze of fresh lemon juice.

*Perfectly Portioned Plate:* Serve with Lemon Garlic Mackerel (page 137).

**Per Serving:** Calories: 115; Fats: 8g; Protein: 4g; Cholesterol: 0mg; Carbohydrates: 12g; Fiber: 5g; Sodium: 266mg

# Roasted Radishes with Rosemary

DAIRY-FREE, GLUTEN-FREE, VEGAN / PREP TIME: 10 MINUTES / COOK TIME: 35 MINUTES

If the earthy, spicy bite of radishes doesn't appeal to you, don't give up on this nutritious vegetable just yet; roasting them completely changes their flavor. The roasting process releases a bit of sweetness and mellows the earthiness, leaving a moist, mild, and versatile vegetable rich in health benefits. A root vegetable related to kale and broccoli, radishes are rich in antioxidant phytochemicals, vitamin C, folate, vitamin $B_6$, and essential minerals, and are very low in calories. And don't throw away the tops—use them in smoothies or sauté them like spinach.

1 bunch radishes, greens intact

1 tablespoon olive oil, plus 1 teaspoon

1 tablespoon chopped fresh rosemary

¼ teaspoon salt

½ teaspoon freshly ground black pepper

1. Preheat the oven to 425°F.

2. Remove the stems from the radishes, separate the leaves from the stems, and set the leaves aside.

3. Cut the radish bulbs into halves or quarters, depending on their size. You want the radishes to be roughly the same size so they roast evenly. Place them in a medium-size bowl.

4. Add 1 tablespoon of olive oil, the rosemary, salt, and pepper to the chopped radishes and toss to coat. Transfer the radishes to a nonstick baking sheet.

5.  Bake for 30 to 35 minutes, or until the radishes are browned and crisp. Remove from the oven.

6.  Meanwhile, in a large sauté pan over medium heat, heat the remaining 1 teaspoon of olive oil. Add the radish leaves and sauté until wilted.

7.  Add the roasted radishes to the pan and toss to combine. Serve immediately.

*Perfectly Portioned Plate:* Serve this side with Balsamic Rosemary Chicken (page 129).

**Per Serving:** Calories: 90; Fats: 10g; Protein: 0g; Cholesterol: 0mg; Carbohydrates: 2g; Fiber: 1g; Sodium: 301mg

Berries with Greek Yogurt Dressing, p. 185

# 10

# Desserts

# Dark Chocolate Avocado Mousse

GLUTEN-FREE / PREP TIME: 10 MINUTES, PLUS 1 HOUR CHILLING TIME

This decadently rich and creamy mousse is full of heart healthy ingredients, and can be prepared in under 10 minutes. Dark chocolate is rich in antioxidants, vitamins, minerals, and a type of phytochemical called polyphenols that can help lower blood pressure and raise good (HDL) cholesterol. Combined with the healthy fats and fiber found in avocados, this thick and nutritious dessert will fill you up and keep you satisfied.

1 large very ripe avocado, peeled and seeded

2 ounces 70% cacao baking chocolate, melted

2 tablespoons unsweetened cocoa powder

¼ cup unsweetened almond milk or nonfat milk

2 tablespoons maple syrup

¼ teaspoon vanilla extract

Pinch ground cinnamon

Pinch salt

1. In a food processor, combine the avocado, melted chocolate, cocoa powder, almond milk, maple syrup, vanilla, cinnamon, and salt and process until smooth. Use less milk for a thicker mousse and more for a thinner consistency.

2. Spoon the mousse into two small ramekins and chill in the refrigerator for at least 1 hour before serving.

**Per Serving:** Calories: 434; Fats: 29g; Protein: 6g; Cholesterol: 7mg; Carbohydrates: 53g; Fiber: 9g; Sodium: 125mg

# Cardamom Apple Almond Crisp

DAIRY-FREE, GLUTEN-FREE / PREP TIME: 10 MINUTES / COOK TIME: 25 MINUTES

This high-fiber crisp is flourless, all natural, low in sugar, and vegan. Apples are high in pectin, a type of soluble fiber beneficial for lowering bad (LDL) cholesterol. Apples are also rich in numerous beneficial phytochemicals and are a good source of the antioxidant vitamin C. For even more cardioprotective benefit, the chewy topping is made from oats and almonds and seasoned with cardamom to make a perfectly portioned light, delicious, and healthy dessert.

Olive oil nonstick cooking spray

*For the fruit*

2 cups chopped unpeeled apples

½ tablespoon brown sugar

1 teaspoon cornstarch

¼ teaspoon ground cardamom

½ teaspoon vanilla extract

*For the topping*

4 tablespoons almonds

3 tablespoons gluten-free rolled oats

1 teaspoon olive oil

1 tablespoon brown sugar

1 teaspoon honey

Pinch salt

Preheat the oven to 400°F and grease two 8-ounce ramekins with cooking spray.

TO PREPARE THE FRUIT

In a medium bowl, stir together the apples, brown sugar, cornstarch, cardamom, and vanilla.

TO MAKE THE TOPPING

1.  In a food processor, process the almonds until finely chopped. Add the oats and pulse until just chopped.

2.  In a small bowl, add the olive oil, brown sugar, honey, and a pinch of salt.

TO PREPARE THE CRISP

1.  Add 2 tablespoons of the topping mixture into the fruit mixture and stir to combine.

2.  Divide the fruit mixture between the prepared ramekins. Sprinkle the rest of the topping over the fruit mixture.

3.  Cover the ramekins with their lids or loosely cover with aluminum foil (the tops will burn if left uncovered).

4.  Bake for 22 to 25 minutes and cool slightly, uncovered, before serving.

**Per Serving:** Calories: 279; Fats: 9g; Protein: 4g; Cholesterol: 0mg; Carbohydrates: 50g; Fiber: 8g; Sodium: 82mg

# Frosted Vanilla Cupcakes

**GLUTEN-FREE, QUICK & EASY / PREP TIME: 10 MINUTES / COOK TIME: 15 MINUTES**

These pretty vanilla cupcakes are that perfect low-calorie, low-fat dessert that makes you think you are eating a higher-calorie bakery treat. The difference is that these are chockfull of nutritious ingredients. Gluten-free oat flour adds cholesterol-lowering soluble fiber, while unsweetened applesauce substitutes added fats and keeps calories in check. Topped with a tangy, lemon–cream cheese frosting, the built-in portion control makes it easy to enjoy a treat without overindulging.

1 egg white

1½ tablespoons brown sugar

1 tablespoon unsweetened applesauce

1 tablespoon olive oil

¾ teaspoon vanilla extract

¼ cup gluten-free oat flour

¼ teaspoon baking powder

Pinch salt

1½ tablespoons nonfat milk or plant-based milk

1 tablespoon nonfat cream cheese, at room temperature

1 teaspoon powdered sugar

½ tablespoon freshly grated lemon zest

1 lemon, halved

¼ cup fresh blueberries, for garnish

1. Preheat the oven to 350°F and spray two cups of a cupcake tin with non-stick cooking spray, or line them with cupcake liners.

2. In a small bowl, whisk together the egg white and brown sugar.

3. Add the applesauce, olive oil, and vanilla and stir to combine. Stir in the flour, baking powder, and salt until combined. Stir in the milk until smooth.

4. Pour into the prepared cups and bake for 10 to 15 minutes, or until cooked through.

5. Meanwhile, stir together the cream cheese, powdered sugar, and lemon zest. Drizzle in just a touch of lemon juice and place the frosting in the refrigerator.

6. Once the cupcakes have cooled, divide the frosting between the two cupcakes, top with fresh blueberries, and serve.

**Per Serving:** Calories: 185; Fats: 6g; Protein: 4g; Cholesterol: 6g; Carbohydrates: 21g; Fiber: 2g; Sodium: 118mg

# Rhubarb Crisp

DAIRY-FREE, GLUTEN-FREE, VEGAN / PREP TIME: 10 MINUTES / COOK TIME: 25 MINUTES

Rhubarb has a plethora of health benefits and is cheap, versatile, and available all year long. Eating healthily doesn't have to be difficult or expensive and enjoying rhubarb regularly can provide you with numerous heart healthy benefits. High in potassium and magnesium, which normalize blood pressure, rhubarb is very low in calories, high in soluble fiber, and contains potent antioxidants and phytochemicals such as anthocyanin, which can reduce your risk of heart disease. The addition of allspice, orange zest, and almond extract to this fruit crisp balances out the tartness of the rhubarb.

*For the filling*
1¼ cups finely diced rhubarb
2 teaspoons gluten-free
    oat flour
3 teaspoons sugar
½ teaspoon almond extract
¼ teaspoon freshly grated
    orange zest
Pinch salt

*For the topping*
3 tablespoons gluten-free
    rolled oats
1 tablespoon packed
    brown sugar
1 tablespoon gluten-free
    oat flour
½ tablespoon olive oil
Pinch ground allspice
Pinch salt

Preheat the oven to 400°F.

TO MAKE THE FILLING

1. In a medium bowl, mix together the rhubarb, flour, sugar, almond extract, orange zest, and salt, stirring well to distribute the orange zest.

2. Pack the filling tightly into two 6-ounce ramekins.

TO MAKE THE TOPPING

1. In a separate bowl, stir together the rolled oats, brown sugar, oat flour, olive oil, allspice, and salt, stirring well to distribute the allspice. Pack the topping on top of the fruit.

2. Place the ramekins on a baking sheet for 20 to 25 minutes, or until the filling is bubbling and the topping is golden brown and crisp. Serve warm.

**Per Serving:** Calories: 137; Fats: 5g; Protein: 2g; Cholesterol: 0g; Carbohydrates: 23g; Fiber: 3g; Sodium: 160mg

# Broiled Mango

**DAIRY-FREE, GLUTEN-FREE, VEGAN, QUICK & EASY / PREP TIME: 5 MINUTES / COOK TIME: 10 MINUTES**

Nothing could be simpler or more nutritious than choosing fresh fruit for dessert. But sometimes it's nice to jazz your fruit up and broiling is the perfect technique for doing that. Broiling makes fruits' inherent sweetness pop and is a cooking technique that works well with just about any fruit. Here, fresh mango, the "king of fruits," is paired with a splash of tart lime juice to balance its sweetness. High in soluble fiber and vitamin C to help lower LDL (bad cholesterol), mangos are rich in vitamin A, $B_6$, potassium, and magnesium.

1 mango, peeled, seeded,
    and sliced
1 lime, cut into wedges

1. Position the rack in the upper third of the oven and preheat the broiler. Line a broiler pan with aluminum foil.

2. Arrange the mango slices in a single layer in the prepared pan. Broil for 8 to 10 minutes, or until browned in spots. Transfer to two plates, squeeze lime wedges over the broiled mango, and serve.

**Per Serving:** Calories: 101; Fats: 1g; Protein: 1g; Cholesterol: 0mg; Carbohydrates: 25g; Fiber: 3g; Sodium: 2mg

# Pumpkin Cakes

DAIRY-FREE, GLUTEN-FREE, VEGAN / PREP TIME: 10 MINUTES / COOK TIME: 25 MINUTES

Cake recipes that serve two are perfect not only for portion control but also for using up those last bits of ingredients, like canned pumpkin purée. This recipe uses ¼ cup of pumpkin purée, an amount often leftover after baking something else. Pumpkin is one of those super nutritious foods that you should consider including in your diet regularly as it is very low in calories, rich in fiber, and is a good source of numerous vitamins and minerals (one serving has more than an entire day's worth of vitamin A). These scrumptious and nutritious cakes can double as a breakfast.

¼ cup canned pumpkin purée

1 tablespoon unsweetened almond milk or nonfat milk

1 tablespoon dark brown sugar

1 tablespoon granulated sugar

1 tablespoon olive oil

½ teaspoon pumpkin pie spice, plus more for garnish

¼ cup gluten-free oat flour

½ teaspoon baking powder

⅛ teaspoon salt

1. Preheat the oven to 350°F.

2. In a small bowl, whisk together the pumpkin purée, almond milk, brown sugar, granulated sugar, olive oil, and pumpkin pie spice.

3. Fold in the flour, baking powder, and salt.

4. Divide the mixture evenly between two 4-ounce ramekins and bake for 24 to 26 minutes, or until a toothpick inserted in the center comes out clean.

5. Serve with an extra dusting of pumpkin pie spice.

**Per Serving:** Calories: 159; Fats: 8g; Protein: 2g; Cholesterol: 0mg; Carbohydrates: 22g; Fiber: 2g; Sodium: 155mg

# Chocolate Cherry "Ice Cream"

DAIRY-FREE, GLUTEN-FREE / PREP TIME: 5 MINUTES, PLUS 1 HOUR CHILLING TIME

While this recipe is not really true "ice cream," you should find this healthy alternative scrumptious in its own right and a sweet dessert that will leave you feeling good. Cherries, chocolate, and avocado come together to produce the same creamy texture and level of taste satisfaction as high-fat, high-sugar ice cream. Avocados are rich in heart healthy fats and fiber, cherries are bursting with protective phytochemicals, and dark chocolate is rich in natural polyphenols important for heart health.

½ avocado, peeled and seeded

1½ cups frozen cherries

2 teaspoons honey

1 pitted date, chopped

1 tablespoon unsweetened cocoa powder

5 tablespoons unsweetened almond milk, plus more as needed, or nonfat milk

1 teaspoon vanilla extract

Pinch salt

Pinch stevia (optional)

1. Add all the ingredients to a food processor and process, scraping down the sides occasionally, for 3 to 5 minutes, or until smooth and the consistency of ice cream.

2. Scoop into a bowl and enjoy immediately or, for a firmer ice cream, transfer to an airtight freezer-safe container and freeze for at least 1 hour.

**Per Serving:** Calories: 215; Fats: 11g; Protein: 4g; Cholesterol: 1mg; Carbohydrates: 30g; Fiber: 7g; Sodium: 103mg

# Frosted Bitter Chocolate Orange Cake

**DAIRY-FREE, GLUTEN-FREE, QUICK & EASY / PREP TIME: 5 MINUTES / COOK TIME: 20 MINUTES**

This treat is made without any added sugars in the cake, and just a touch of maple syrup added to the creamy peanut butter frosting. Baked in small ramekins, the cake is made from oat flour and has a moist, soft texture resembling true cake. The lightly sweetened frosting is made from natural peanut butter, adding healthy fats and heart healthy vitamin E. High in protein, low in sodium, and high in fiber, this bit of chocolate bliss is as delicious as it is nutritious.

*For the cake*

5 tablespoons gluten-free
    oat flour
2 tablespoons unsweetened
    cocoa
¼ teaspoon baking powder
Pinch salt
1 egg
2 teaspoons olive oil
1 tablespoon unsweetened
    applesauce
1 tablespoon freshly squeezed
    orange juice
1 teaspoon freshly grated
    orange zest

*For the peanut butter frosting*

1½ tablespoons natural
    unsweetened peanut butter
1 tablespoon freshly squeezed
    orange juice
1 to 2 tablespoons nonfat
    or plant-based milk
½ teaspoon vanilla extract
1 teaspoon maple syrup
Pinch ground cinnamon

TO MAKE THE CAKE

1.  Preheat the oven to 350°F.

2.  In a small bowl, mix together the cake ingredients.

3.  Divide the batter between two well-oiled 4-ounce ramekins.

4.  Bake the cakes for 15 to 20 minutes until springy to the touch.

TO MAKE THE PEANUT BUTTER FROSTING

1.  In a small bowl, whisk together the ingredients for the frosting, adding more milk if necessary to reach your desired consistency.

2.  Let the cakes cool for a few minutes, remove them from the ramekins, spread the frosting over the tops, and enjoy.

**Per Serving:** Calories: 240; Fats: 15g; Protein: 9g; Cholesterol: 82mg; Carbohydrates: 22g; Fiber: 4g; Sodium: 174mg

# Marsala-Poached Figs over Ricotta

GLUTEN-FREE, QUICK & EASY / PREP TIME: 5 MINUTES / COOK TIME: 5 MINUTES

This elegant and heart healthy dessert is made using figs, a fruit rich in the mineral potassium that helps control blood pressure. Figs are also a good source of dietary fiber and vitamin $B_6$, which helps keep homocysteine levels in check. Poaching the figs in Marsala wine adds beneficial phytochemicals and a rich taste, and low-fat ricotta cheese provides a creamy yet nutritious counterbalance. Decadently tasty, this recipe can be made in 10 minutes.

½ cup quartered dried figs

¼ cup Marsala or port

2 teaspoons honey

½ cup part-skim ricotta cheese

½ teaspoon granulated stevia, or 1 teaspoon sugar

¼ teaspoon vanilla extract

1½ tablespoons toasted slivered almonds

1. Place the figs, Marsala, and honey in a small saucepan. Bring to a boil, decrease the heat, and simmer for 5 minutes, or until the figs soften and the wine is syrupy.

2. Meanwhile, in a small bowl, stir together the ricotta, stevia, and vanilla. Divide between two bowls, top with the fig mixture and the almonds, and serve.

**Per Serving:** Calories: 290; Fats: 8g; Protein: 10g; Cholesterol: 19mg; Carbohydrates: 45g; Fiber: 5g; Sodium: 84mg

# Berries with Greek Yogurt Dressing

**GLUTEN-FREE, QUICK & EASY / PREP TIME: 5 MINUTES**

Creamy, sweet, lip-smackingly good, and with no artificial sweeteners, this high-protein, calcium-rich, honey yogurt sauce is perfect on fruit for a nutritious dessert that takes 5 minutes to make. Full of anti-inflammatory phytochemicals and cholesterol-lowering fiber, berries are some of the most nutritious foods you can include in your heart healthy diet. An easy way to do this is to make it a habit to include berries once a day by having them as a snack or dessert. Topping the berries with a Greek yogurt dressing adds satiating protein, making the dessert even more satisfying. For peak nutrition, try to use berries that are in season.

2 cups mixed berries
   (raspberries, blueberries,
   cherries)
1 cup plain nonfat
   Greek yogurt
¼ cup honey
½ teaspoon vanilla extract
Pinch ground cinnamon

1. Wash the berries in a colander and portion into two serving dishes.

2. In a small bowl, combine the Greek yogurt, honey, vanilla, and cinnamon and whisk until fully combined.

3. Top each dish of berries with half of the yogurt dressing.

4. Enjoy immediately.

**Per Serving:** Calories: 283; Fats: 2g; Protein: 9g; Cholesterol: 7mg; Carbohydrates: 59g; Fiber: 8g; Sodium: 89mg

Salsa Verde, p. 197

# 11

# Staples

# Homemade Ketchup

DAIRY-FREE, GLUTEN-FREE, QUICK & EASY / MAKES 1½ CUPS, SERVING SIZE 1 TABLESPOON
PREP TIME: 5 MINUTES / COOK TIME: 5 MINUTES

When you are following a low-sodium diet, you start to realize that hidden salt is in just about everything, and condiments are no exception. Ketchup from the big companies also contains highly processed corn syrup as a sweetener, along with other preservatives. Not only is making your own ketchup easier than you think, but it also gives you control over how much sugar, salt, and other ingredients you add. Plus homemade just tastes better and you can even customize it with your favorite spices.

1 (6-ounce) can tomato paste, no salt added

½ cup cider vinegar

2 tablespoons honey

1 teaspoon liquid smoke

2 teaspoons garlic powder

2 teaspoons onion powder

½ teaspoon freshly ground black pepper

½ teaspoon ground cloves

½ teaspoon ground ginger

½ teaspoon ground oregano

½ teaspoon smoked paprika

1 cup water

1. In a small bowl, whisk together the tomato paste, vinegar, honey, liquid smoke, garlic powder, onion powder, pepper, cloves, ginger, oregano, and paprika.

2. Whisk in ½ cup of water until fully incorporated. Add the remaining water 1 tablespoon at a time until you reach your desired consistency of ketchup.

**Per Serving:** Calories: 14; Fats: 0g; Protein: 0g; Cholesterol: 0mg; Carbohydrates: 3g; Fiber: 0g; Sodium: 8mg

# Avocado Salsa

DAIRY-FREE, GLUTEN-FREE, VEGAN, QUICK & EASY / MAKES 2 ½ CUPS, SERVING SIZE 2 TABLESPOONS
PREP TIME: 5 MINUTES

Salsas are a great low-fat, low-calorie topping, but processed salsa is preserved with sodium, and an average brand contains over 400 milligrams of sodium per 2-tablespoon serving! If you are generous with your salsa portions, you can see how that can be a problem on a low-sodium diet. This nutritious homemade salsa recipe uses heart healthy avocados, fresh tomatoes, and pantry spices to create a delicious dip that saves you hundreds of milligrams of sodium per serving.

5 Roma tomatoes, chopped

3 avocados, peeled, pitted, and cubed

½ cup chopped red onion

4 tablespoons chopped fresh cilantro

2 garlic cloves, minced

Juice of ½ lime

¼ teaspoon salt

⅛ teaspoon freshly ground black pepper

Dash sriracha sauce

In a medium mixing bowl, mix together the tomatoes, avocados, red onion, cilantro, and garlic. Add the lime juice, salt, pepper, and sriracha and mix well. Serve immediately.

**Per Serving:** Calories: 69; Fats: 6g; Protein: 1g; Cholesterol: 0mg; Carbohydrates: 4g; Fiber: 3g; Sodium: 35mg

# Spaghetti Sauce

DAIRY-FREE, GLUTEN-FREE, VEGAN / MAKES 3½ CUPS, SERVING SIZE ½ CUP / PREP TIME: 5 MINUTES
COOK TIME: 35 MINUTES

Skip the processed jarred spaghetti sauce and make your own flavorful, chunky, homemade sauce without the addition of loads of sodium or refined sugars. With added phytochemicals and fiber from fresh onions and minced garlic, this recipe uses basic pantry staples and seasonings and is quick to put together. Add your favorite protein such as lean chicken breast, beans, or lean beef, and use the sauce just as you would regular spaghetti sauce—spoon over zucchini noodles, whole-grain pasta, or grains like quinoa and brown rice.

Olive oil nonstick
  cooking spray
¼ cup chopped onion
3 garlic cloves, minced
1 (15-ounce) can tomato sauce,
  no salt added
½ cup tomato paste,
  no salt added
1½ cups water
½ teaspoon unsweetened
  cocoa (optional)
2 tablespoons dried basil
2 teaspoons dried oregano
½ teaspoon red pepper flakes
⅛ teaspoon salt
Freshly ground black pepper

1. Spray a large skillet with cooking spray and heat over medium heat. Add the onion and garlic to the skillet and sauté for 4 to 5 minutes, or until fragrant and translucent.

2. Add the tomato sauce, tomato paste, and water and stir to combine.

3. Add the cocoa (if using), basil, oregano, red pepper flakes, salt, and a few grinds of pepper and simmer on low for 20 to 30 minutes. Serve over pasta, grains, or vegetables.

*Tip:* Add optional protein when the spices are added.

**Per Serving:** Calories: 36; Fats: 0g; Protein: 2g; Cholesterol: 0mg; Carbohydrates: 8g; Fiber: 2g; Sodium: 98mg

# Italian Salad Dressing

DAIRY-FREE, GLUTEN-FREE, VEGAN, QUICK & EASY / MAKES ½ CUP, SERVING SIZE 1 TABLESPOON
PREP TIME: 5 MINUTES

This quick and easy recipe for low-sodium Italian salad dressing can be made in just minutes and doesn't contain any added sugars or salt. Using heart healthy olive oil, which is rich in cholesterol-lowering monounsaturated fats, and a handful of herbs and spices, you can create a flavorful dressing for salads, sandwiches, cooked vegetables, grains, and proteins. This recipe is easy to customize with your favorite herbs and spices and can be prepared up to a day ahead of time.

3 tablespoons olive oil

2 tablespoons red wine vinegar

1 tablespoon freshly squeezed
   lemon juice

2 teaspoons Dijon mustard

2 garlic cloves, minced

1 teaspoon dried basil

1 teaspoon dried parsley

¼ teaspoon dried oregano

⅛ teaspoon red pepper flakes

Pinch freshly ground
   black pepper

Combine all the ingredients in a jar with a screw cap, cover, and shake to blend. Store in the refrigerator.

**Per Serving:** Calories: 48; Fats: 3g; Protein: 0g; Cholesterol: 0mg; Carbohydrates: 0g; Fiber: 0g; Sodium: 15mg

# Creamy Maple-Dijon Dressing

GLUTEN-FREE, QUICK & EASY / MAKES ¼ CUP, SERVING SIZE 1 TABLESPOON / PREP TIME: 5 MINUTES

This salad dressing is full of flavor, with a smooth, rich texture that is lightened by using nutritious, high-protein Greek yogurt, a healthy substitute for high-fat dressing ingredients such as mayonnaise and sour cream. A touch of maple syrup is matched with Dijon mustard to produce a dressing with sweet and tangy notes. This quick vinaigrette is very low in sodium and added fats, making it a heart healthy choice, and is a fantastic addition to slightly bitter salad greens like kale or arugula.

½ cup plain nonfat
   Greek yogurt
¼ cup Dijon mustard
1 tablespoon apple cider
   vinegar
1 tablespoon maple syrup
1 tablespoon olive oil
Pinch salt
Pinch freshly ground
   black pepper

Place all the ingredients in a bowl and whisk together, or add to a jar with a lid and shake vigorously until thoroughly combined. Use immediately and store any unused portion in the refrigerator for up to 5 days.

**Per Serving:** Calories: 25; Fats: 2g; Protein: 1g; Cholesterol: 1mg; Carbohydrates: 2g; Fiber: 0g; Sodium: 78mg

# Lime Glaze

DAIRY-FREE, QUICK & EASY / MAKES ½ CUP, SERVING SIZE 2 TABLESPOONS
PREP TIME: 1 MINUTE / COOK TIME: 2 MINUTES

If you have been searching for a low-fat way to add flavor to chicken, fish, and vegetables, then look no further. This tangy lime glaze adds a citrus flavor and moisture without additional fat. While the recipe is low in sugar, you could reduce it even further by replacing the sugar with granulated stevia. It's also easy to customize with your favorite herbs and spices and vary the type of broth—vegetable, beef, or fish—depending on the dish you're making.

½ cup unsalted chicken broth

1 teaspoon freshly squeezed lime juice

1 teaspoon freshly grated lime zest

2 tablespoons chopped fresh parsley

¼ teaspoon garlic powder

¼ teaspoon onion powder

1 tablespoon sugar

2 teaspoons cornstarch

1. In a microwavable bowl, whisk together all the ingredients.

2. Microwave on high for 1 to 2 minutes, or until the glaze is clear and thickened.

**Per Serving:** Calories: 23; Fats: 0g; Protein: 1g; Cholesterol: 0mg; Carbohydrates: 5g; Fiber: 3g; Sodium: 97mg

# Roasted Red Pepper Sauce

**DAIRY-FREE, GLUTEN-FREE, VEGAN / SERVES 4 / PREP TIME: 15 MINUTES / COOK TIME: 50 MINUTES**

This creamy, savory-sweet red pepper sauce is light, healthy, and simple yet incredibly satisfying. Using red bell peppers and basic pantry staples, this gourmet-tasting sauce is sumptuous with whole-wheat pasta, chicken, fish, grains, beans, or vegetables. Red bell peppers are an excellent source of the antioxidant vitamins C and A, and contain numerous phytochemicals that can reduce inflammation in the body. Low in calories, fat, and sodium, the combination of ingredients provides the perfect balance of savory, sweet, and heat, while fresh parsley adds a touch of freshness.

2 red bell peppers

1 tablespoon olive oil

2 shallots, finely chopped

4 garlic cloves, finely chopped

Salt

Freshly ground black pepper

1½ cups unsweetened almond milk or nonfat milk

2 tablespoons nutritional yeast

1½ tablespoons cornstarch or arrowroot powder

Pinch red pepper flakes

2 tablespoons chopped fresh parsley

1. Heat the oven to 500°F.

2. Roast the bell peppers on a baking sheet for 25 to 30 minutes, or until charred. Cover in aluminum foil for 10 minutes to steam, then peel away the charred skin. Halve the bell peppers and remove the stems and seeds. Set them aside.

3. While the peppers are roasting, heat the olive oil in a large skillet over medium heat. Add the shallots and garlic and sauté for 4 to 5 minutes, or until golden brown and soft. Season with salt and pepper.

4. Transfer the sautéed shallot and garlic to a blender with the roasted peppers, almond milk, nutritional yeast, cornstarch, red pepper flakes, and parsley. Blend until creamy and smooth, taste, and adjust the seasonings as needed.

5. Once blended, transfer the sauce back to the skillet and heat over medium heat to thicken. Once simmering, decrease the heat to low and simmer for 4 to 5 minutes, or until the sauce is thickened to your desired consistency. Serve immediately.

**Per Serving:** Calories: 116; Fats: 4g; Protein: 8g; Cholesterol: 2mg; Carbohydrates: 14g; Fiber: 2g; Sodium: 95mg

# Seasoned Rice Mix

VEGAN, QUICK & EASY / MAKES 6 CUPS OF DRY MIX, SERVING SIZE ¼ CUP / PREP TIME: 5 MINUTES

Boxed rice mix may be convenient, but these products offer little more than refined grains and lots of excess sodium. Eating a one-cup portion of rice prepared according to package directions (including prepackaged seasonings and added margarine) can provide up to 1,350 mg of sodium. Compare that to the Dietary Guidelines for Americans recommended limit of 2,300 mg per day and you are well on your way to sodium overload. You can solve that problem by making your own much more nutritious, virtually sodium-free rice mix to keep on hand for a quick and easy whole-grain side dish.

4 cups uncooked instant brown rice

2 tablespoons vegetable-flavored low-sodium bouillon granules

2 tablespoons dried parsley

½ cup dried vegetable flakes

2 teaspoons crushed dried rosemary

1 teaspoon dried marjoram

1 teaspoon dried thyme

1 teaspoon garlic powder

1 teaspoon onion powder

½ teaspoon freshly ground black pepper

1. In a medium bowl, mix together the rice, bouillon, parsley, vegetable flakes, rosemary, marjoram, thyme, garlic powder, onion powder, and pepper. Store in an airtight container.

2. To make the seasoned rice, use a ratio of 1 cup mix to 1 cup boiling water, simmer for 5 minutes, remove from the heat, and stir. Cover the rice and let it stand for 5 minutes. Fluff with a fork before serving.

**Per Serving:** Calories: 116; Fats: 1g; Protein: 2g; Cholesterol: 0mg; Carbohydrates: 25g; Fiber: 1g; Sodium: 89mg

# Sherried Mushroom Sauce

QUICK & EASY / MAKES 3 CUPS, SERVING SIZE ¼ CUP / PREP TIME: 5 MINUTES
COOK TIME: 12 MINUTES

The rich flavor of this nutritious and hearty mushroom and sherry sauce is intensely satisfying. Mushrooms are high in cholesterol-lowering fiber, and are a good source of vitamin D, in addition to numerous anti-inflammatory phytochemicals. Try this sauce over chicken, roasted vegetables, and cooked grains.

2 cups nonfat milk

2 teaspoons olive oil

1 small onion, diced

1 cup sliced button mushrooms

1 cup sliced cremini mushrooms

2 tablespoons whole-wheat flour

1 tablespoon chopped fresh chives

Freshly ground black pepper

1 teaspoon sherry

1. In a small saucepan, warm the milk over medium heat.

2. Heat the olive oil in a medium nonstick skillet over medium heat. Add the onion to the skillet and sauté for about 3 minutes. Add the button and cremini mushrooms and sauté for another 3 minutes. Stir in the flour and continue to cook for another 2 to 3 minutes.

3. Whisk in the warmed milk and continue to cook, stirring frequently, for about 3 minutes, or until thickened. Add the chives, season with pepper, pour in the sherry, stir, and serve over the dish of your choice.

**Per Serving:** Calories: 33; Fats: 1g; Protein: 2g; Cholesterol: 1mg; Carbohydrates: 4g; Fiber: 3g; Sodium: 23mg

# Salsa Verde

DAIRY-FREE, GLUTEN-FREE, VEGAN, QUICK & EASY / MAKES 2 ½ CUPS, SERVING SIZE 2 TABLESPOONS
PREP TIME: 10 MINUTES / COOK TIME: 10 MINUTES

The green ingredient in salsa verde that adds a spicy tart flavor, the tomatillo, offers a number of heart healthy benefits. Low in calories, a one-cup serving provides over 20 percent of the daily value for the antioxidant vitamin C, almost 3 grams of fiber, and high amounts of niacin and potassium, which promote healthy cholesterol and blood pressure levels. Discover how simple it is to make this fresh salsa verde by preparing this recipe, then use it as a topping for sweet potatoes, burritos, eggs, frittatas, and breakfast tacos, or enjoy as a dip with whole-grain corn chips.

1½ pounds tomatillos (about 12 medium), husked and rinsed

1 medium jalapeño, stemmed (omit for mild salsa, use 2 for hot salsa)

½ cup chopped red onion

⅓ cup chopped fresh cilantro

2 tablespoons freshly squeezed lime juice

¼ teaspoon salt

2 garlic cloves

1. Preheat the broiler and position a rack about 4 inches below the heat source. Place the tomatillos and jalapeño on a rimmed baking sheet and broil until they are blackened in spots, about 5 minutes.

2. Remove the baking sheet from the oven, carefully flip over the tomatillos and jalapeño with tongs and broil for 4 to 6 more minutes, until the tomatillos are splotchy-black and blistered.

3. Meanwhile, in a food processor or blender, combine the onion, cilantro, lime juice, salt, and garlic. Once the tomatillos are out of the oven, carefully transfer the hot tomatillos, jalapeño, and all of their juices into the food processor or blender.

4. Pulse until the mixture is mostly smooth and no big chunks of tomatillo remain, scraping down the sides as necessary. Season with additional lime juice if desired.

**Per Serving (¼ cup):** Calories: 26; Fats: 1g; Protein: 1g; Cholesterol: 0mg; Carbohydrates: 5g; Fiber: 2g; Sodium: 60mg

# Glossary

**Antioxidant:** A substance such as vitamin E, vitamin C, or beta-carotene, thought to protect the body cells from the damaging effects of oxidation.

**Atherosclerosis:** A common form of arteriosclerosis in which fatty substances form a deposit of plaque on the inner lining of arterial walls.

**FIFO:** First In, First Out. It simply means a system of labeling foods with the dates that you purchase them or want to use them by, and putting the older foods in front or on top so that you use them first.

**HDL cholesterol:** A blood-plasma lipoprotein that is composed of a high proportion of protein with little triglyceride and cholesterol and that is correlated with reduced risk of atherosclerosis. Also called good cholesterol.

**LDL cholesterol:** A blood-plasma lipoprotein that is high in cholesterol and low in protein content and that carries cholesterol to cells and tissues. Also called bad cholesterol.

**Phytochemical/Phytonutrient:** A non-nutritive bioactive plant substance, such as a flavonoid or carotenoid, considered to have a beneficial effect on human health.

**Ramekin:** A small ceramic bowl for baking and serving.

# References

Centers for Disease Control and Prevention. Heart Disease. Updated November 8, 2016. Accessed November 9, 2016. www.cdc.gov/heartdisease.

DASH Eating Plan. National Heart, Lung, and Blood Institute. Updated September 16, 2015. Accessed November 7, 2016. www.nhlbi.nih.gov/health/health-topics/topics/dash.

Eckel, R. H., J. M. Jakicic, J. D. Ard, V. S. Hubbard, J. M. de Jesus, et al. "2013 AHA/ACC Guideline on Lifestyle Management to Reduce Cardiovascular Risk." *Circulation*, 2013; Accessed November 7, 2016. circ.ahajournals.org/content/early/2013/11/11/01.cir.0000437740.48606.d1.10ng.

Harvard T. H. Chan School of Public Health. Healthy Dietary Styles. 2016. Accessed November 9, 2016. www.hsph.harvard.edu/nutritionsource/healthy-dietary-styles/.

*Health.gov.* 2008 Physical Activity Guidelines for Americans. ODPHP. Accessed November 8, 2016. health.gov/paguidelines/guidelines/.

*Health.gov.* 2015–2020 Dietary Guidelines for Americans. ODPHP. Accessed November 8, 2016. health.gov/dietaryguidelines/2015/.

The American Heart Association. Nutrition. Updated October 24, 2016. Accessed November 7, 2016. www.heart.org/HEARTORG/HealthyLiving/HealthyEating/Nutrition/Nutrition_UCM_310436_SubHomePage.jsp.

Therapeutic Lifestyle Changes (TLC) for High Cholesterol. WebMd.com. Accessed November 9, 2016. www.webmd.com/cholesterol-management/tc/therapeutic-lifestyle-changes-tlc-diet-for-high-cholesterol-#1.

University of Maryland Medical Center. Heart-healthy Diet. Accessed November 7, 2016. umm.edu/health/medical/reports/articles/hearthealthy-diet.

U.S. News and World Report. Best Diet Rankings. Accessed November 9, 2016. health.usnews.com/best-diet.

World's Healthiest Foods. Accessed November 7, 2016. www.whfoods.com/.

# Resources

Academy of Nutrition and Dietetics. Heart and Cardiovascular Health. www.eatright.org/resources/health/wellness/heart-and-cardiovascular-health.

American Heart Association. The American Heart Association's Diet and Lifestyle Recommendations. www.heart.org/HEARTORG/HealthyLiving/HealthyEating/Nutrition/The-American-Heart-Associations-Diet-and-Lifestyle-Recommendations_UCM_305855_Article.jsp#.WDtH-qIrJ-U.

American Heart Association. Nutrition. www.heart.org/HEARTORG/HealthyLiving/HealthyEating/Nutrition/Nutrition_UCM_310436_SubHomePage.jsp.

American Heart Association. "Simple Cooking and Recipes." recipes.heart.org.Health.gov. 2015-2020 Dietary Guidelines for Americans. health.gov/dietaryguidelines/2015/.

Mayo Clinic. "Mediterranean Diet: A Heart Healthy Eating Plan." www.mayoclinic.org/healthy-lifestyle/nutrition-and-healthy-eating/in-depth/mediterranean-diet/art-20047801.

Million Hearts, Centers for Disease Control and Prevention. "Healthy Eating and Lifestyle Resource Center." recipes.millionhearts.hhs.gov/.

National Heart, Lung, and Blood Institute. DASH Eating Plan. www.nhlbi.nih.gov/health/health-topics/topics/dash.

Nutrition.gov. Heart Health. https://www.nutrition.gov/nutrition-and-health-issues/heart-health.

Seconds Count.org. "Nutrition, Diet & Your Heart." www.secondscount.org/healthy-living/heart-healthy-nutrition-diet#.WDtlAqIrJ-U.

Therapeutic Lifestyle Changes (TLC) for High Cholesterol. WebMd.com. www.webmd.com/cholesterol-management/tc/therapeutic-lifestyle-changes-tlc-diet-for-high-cholesterol-#1

University of Maryland Medical Center. Heart-healthy Diet. http://umm.edu/health/medical/reports/articles/hearthealthy-diet.

# Measurement Conversions

## Volume Equivalents (Dry)

| US STANDARD | METRIC (APPROXIMATE) |
|---|---|
| ⅛ teaspoon | 0.5 mL |
| ¼ teaspoon | 1 mL |
| ½ teaspoon | 2 mL |
| ¾ teaspoon | 4 mL |
| 1 teaspoon | 5 mL |
| 1 tablespoon | 15 mL |
| ¼ cup | 59 mL |
| ⅓ cup | 79 mL |
| ½ cup | 118 mL |
| ⅔ cup | 156 mL |
| ¾ cup | 177 mL |
| 1 cup | 235 mL |
| 2 cups or 1 pint | 475 mL |
| 3 cups | 700 mL |
| 4 cups or 1 quart | 1 L |
| ½ gallon | 2 L |
| 1 gallon | 4 L |

## Volume Equivalents (Liquid)

| US STANDARD | US STANDARD (OUNCES) | METRIC (APPROXIMATE) |
|---|---|---|
| 2 tablespoons | 1 fl. oz. | 30 mL |
| ¼ cup | 2 fl. oz. | 60 mL |
| ½ cup | 4 fl. oz. | 120 mL |
| 1 cup | 8 fl. oz. | 240 mL |
| 1½ cups | 12 fl. oz. | 355 mL |
| 2 cups or 1 pint | 16 fl. oz. | 475 mL |
| 4 cups or 1 quart | 32 fl. oz. | 1 L |
| 1 gallon | 128 fl. oz. | 4 L |

## Oven Temperatures

| FAHRENHEIT (F) | CELSIUS (C) (APPROXIMATE) |
|---|---|
| 250°F | 120°C |
| 300°F | 150°C |
| 325°F | 165°C |
| 350°F | 180°C |
| 375°F | 190°C |
| 400°F | 200°C |
| 425°F | 220°C |
| 450°F | 230°C |

# Index

# About the Author

**Jennifer Koslo** is a registered dietitian nutritionist (RDN), board certified specialist in sports dietetics (CSSD), licensed dietitian in Texas, and an American Council on Exercise certified personal trainer. A member of the Sports, Cardiovascular, and Wellness Practice Group of the Academy of Nutrition and Dietetics (SCAN), she holds a PhD in education and a dual MS in Exercise Science and Human Nutrition. Jennifer's experience includes spending almost three years as a U.S. Peace Corps volunteer in Sierra Leone, West Africa; working in clinical nutrition as a cardiac dietitian; and serving as the chronic disease nutritionist for a state health department, as a college professor teaching nutrition and sports nutrition, and as a private practice dietitian doing one-on-one nutrition counseling. Author of four healthy eating cookbooks: *The 21-Day Healthy Smoothie Plan*, *Diabetic Cooking for Two*, *The Healthy Smoothie Recipe Book*, and *The Alkaline Diet for Beginners*, Jennifer continues to teach college-level nutrition and sports nutrition, writes, and provides individual nutrition counseling and personal training services.